Finding Your Crack
In The Market

Finding Your Crack In The Market

Small Business Secrets to Marketing Niche Dominance and Wealth Creation

Ron Burgess

My sincere thanks to Linda Steiner, Ph.D., University of Maryland, for her guidance.

Book design by RedFusion Media

Book cover design by Cindy Barents

Published By RedFusion Media, Inc. Redlands California USA

ISBN 978-0-9884887-0-0

The book is intended to provide authoritative information in regard to the subject matter covered. The content of this book should not be understood as rendering legal, investment, accounting or other professional services.

Website: www.FindingYourCrack.com

**Dedicated to my friend and mentor,
Don Griffith, Jr.**

Finding Your Crack in the Market

Table of Contents

Why I Wrote This Book

Small business has always been the bedrock of America's standard of living. It is the engine driving the economy and innovation. After every modern recession, small business historically has led the economy back to health by being the first to hire workers. Indeed small businesses create the vast majority of jobs in the private sector—some 67%, for those companies with between 20 and 499 employees, according to the Bureau of Labor Statistics.

Several decades ago when I was in business school, most business schools focused on managing someone else's money, in the form of the large corporation. I was interested in small business, so I tried to adapt what I learned about balance sheets, management, human resources and production management to the small organization.

In 1972 I launched a specialty retail store with my mentors. I remember the exact day I went over to my business textbook shelf to look up an accounting issue. It was five years later, in 1977! The realization then, and my life's work as a business consultant since, is that *small business does not run like big business.* In other words, small business is not big business only small.

Oh, I tried to turn my store (which eventually grew to seven stores) into a well-managed and profitable business. What I got instead was a top heavy, regimented organization that focused on inventory turnover, sales volume, and airtight financials. Being in the fashion industry, we did enjoy ample creativity. We needed that, if we were going to survive. I learned years later, however, as a consultant *to* retailers, that my former business was much heavier in administration than almost all similar small retail chains.

That degree and kind of administration was not a particularly bad thing. Small businesses do benefit from good management. Nevertheless, after thirty years as a consultant, I now know that *efficient management and administration do not correlate with small business success.* Having worked with many successful businesses over the years, I have seen close up how their owners can be disorganized, have behavioral issues, and even distract their employees from performing their assigned activities, yet still succeed.

At first, this seemed to me to be incongruent. But I continued to read the best work on large and small business, openly discuss these issues with my colleagues, and carefully observe real results from both successful and failing businesses. And gradually I began to carefully sort out the characteristics of successful small businesses. During the last ten years or so, as I have watched clients and worked to carefully position their companies, I have learned what really does work and why it works.

I actively keep up on business trends, and have seen good people talk around the edges of the issues at the heart of *Finding Your Crack in The*

Market. Most marketing consultants write a plan and then simply move on to the next client. Even expert marketing executives stay with a company for only an average of just 22 months. As a result, few marketing professionals see the results of their plans – what worked and what didn't. Most of the authors producing books on this subject are addressing the large-scale business audience, or are forced to write from a theoretical or academic perspective simply because they don't have the very long-term laboratory that I have had at my disposal, with many, many years of intimate knowledge of companies.

This is the reason for the book: I have not seen these marketing strategy principles articulated or presented to small business. For some time, I have kept the principles to myself. After all, this knowledge was my own market differentiator. But wanting to wind down a sometimes hectic practice and prompted by colleagues to pass this wisdom along, I have placed these concepts in this book. Frankly, I'm a little uncomfortable writing anything that so clearly takes issue with typical marketing practices. (As you will see, I challenge the idea that conventional assumptions and strategies designed for big businesses work well for small business.) On the other hand, much of how contemporary marketing is designed and implemented is done for the wrong reasons, or has no reason at all. I believe small business owners, or would-be owners, should know what has made the successful ones successful. They should understand when and how they need marketing, and what marketing can accomplish. This book explains precisely those issues for people who are seeking to launch a small business, for people who have launched a small business and for successful business people who want to create growth and wealth.

Why Should You Believe Me?

Good question indeed. These days, when everyone can be a writer, knowing about the author you are reading is important. Too many authors just spout off on every subject. Too few can back up their statements and perspectives with evidence and analysis. So I have carefully considered this question and have hoped to explain specifically why reading this perspective is worth your time. It is important for you to know about where I have been.

Unlike many writers I admire, (Jack Trout, Al Ries, Michael Porter, Tom Peters, Jim Collins, Alvin Toffler and many more) I am not an intellectual. My background is different. I studied biology for three years, but realized that I did not have the smarts to succeed in medical school. Frustrated, I added up the hours I had toward a BA and found that the quickest way to finish was in the design arts. Artists and designers in the 1960s were paid just above minimum wage. So I transferred into the School of Business in the first semester of my fifth year. With the benefit of six years of school, including four summer sessions, I graduated with a BA in Art that semester and a BS in Business the following year. This was not the conventional route at the University of Colorado: undergraduates were supposed to leave and later reapply for a master's program. My move was counter to policy. Luckily, large administrations being what they are, they never found out and I got two degrees.

By the time I finished my B.S. in Business, I also had coursework in economics, calculus, accounting, and management. I had taken science, fine art, business and education courses. (I thought I might need to teach biology or art at some point.) A scholar this does not make me. But most people would probably agree that I was well rounded.

To say that I did not have the typical business student profile is an understatement. My business "coat and tie" classmates often observed me in finance class, having arrived directly from the pottery throwing class, with potting mud running from one ankle to the crotch of my jeans and back down the other leg! Yes, I got strange looks from the prof.

I had grown up in an upper-middle class professional family, with no exposure to business. So, as a sophomore struggling in biology, I began to think about business school. I decided to learn firsthand, and test out the idea before transferring, by working in a real business. I began this process as a summer job following my second year of college. The local men's store "on the Hill" in Boulder, The Regiment, really wanted fraternity men. I was a houseboy at the Delta Gamma sorority. (Here was a job I loved!) So I bypassed The Regiment and went straight to one of Boulder's "cooler" shops, Boot Hill, and made my case.

I thought the interview with Don Griffith, Jr. went pretty well, so the next weekend, when my dad visited the campus, we walked by the store. Don told me, years later, that I said, "Dad, this is where I'm going to work so I'll have real experience for business school." I did not realize that Don was standing to the side of the open door and could hear the entire conversation. In any case, I was offered the job after that stroke of good luck, and managed to schedule work around my courses.

Campus life was changing rapidly during the late sixties and so was fashion. In just four years, students at CU went from wearing coats and ties—even at football games—to wearing torn bell-bottom jeans and lightweight hiking boots, famously known as clutter boots. This made campus fashion retail exciting. I was in the middle of an explosion of change. Fashion came from the campus and, through rock and roll, influenced the entire world. Berkeley and Boulder were at the epicenter of these fashion changes.

Don Griffith, Jr. was a genius at studying people in order to extrapolate the next fashion trends. I carefully watched and learned from him. He taught me how to sell on the floor (an art that is now gone except perhaps at Nordstrom's). And I received another bonus: Don Griffith,Sr. was behind the scenes. He had been one of the early MBA's in the country, with a master's degree in business. He graduated in about 1924. Mr. G, as we called him, had years of retail business experience to draw from, including thriving downtown department stores like Herbergers in Minnesota and Sears Roebuck. During World War II, as a member of a rationing board he controlled footwear and soft goods that retailers required. They needed to use rationing coupons from customers to re-purchase new goods to replace their skimpy inventory. Don Jr. had also been a salesman in retail, after the war. He and Mr. G started a tiny shoe store in Boulder, Colorado.

Mr. G set up the store's manual accounting system. Remember this was before computers and before calculators. In the late 1960s, we used an adding machine to balance the cash registers, manually categorized what we sold, and recorded every sale in a huge columnar pad. This was the key "database" about product movement and trends. It was necessary so we knew more about how to buy. We also recorded the weather, and unusual events that could influence the next year's buy. (Among such events that affected business were the war protest riots with minor looting, during which we had broken windows. I was pleased to be chosen from all the employees to record this information, and do the cash register balancing and check out during their vacations. It took me years to appreciate what a bonanza this was for learning about small business. I saw the art (Don's fashion sense) and the science (Mr. G's deep experience in business management) of business. The experience eventually meshed with my formal business education.

Soon, I became a manager responsible for hiring, training and scheduling the Boot Hill sales team. With both Jr. and Sr. coaching me, I was the beneficiary of a fast-track management program. It was a small part-time job, but I did well financially. Or at least it seemed to me that I was making lots of money as a manager.

As a student, I had few expenses. Because I ate at the Delta Gamma house and shared low rent with five other guys, I was able to save. Indeed, having noticed the large boarding house next to the DG house was for sale, I investigated. It had four sleeping rooms upstairs with a shared bath and two large apartments. I had the down payment in the bank, and went ahead and I bought it. This way I could live in it and eliminate my own rent. Because I was still just 20 but needed to be 21 to own property, I had to bring my parents into the deal. It was prime rental property. I painted the rooms in the summer and rented it at the start of the year. I kept it for a year or so after I graduated, and did quite well for the times, with about a 30% increase in value, and 30% ROI each year on the investment.

Upon graduating from CU, I started looking for jobs. At that point, Don Jr. and Sr. offered me a partnership in a specialty store next to the University of Denver campus. Initially we sold men's and women's footwear, then later added leather goods and some sportswear.

Together Don and I created many design innovations in footwear that increased business and built brand. Some of the innovations that we are most proud of include the FRYE Harness Boot (which is now listed by Footwear News as one of the 10 footwear classics of all time); the first navy blue hiking boots; and many new sandal designs.

Plus we were the first in Denver to carry Nikes. This may seem implausible now, but at the time, Nike founder Phil Knight was known only as an athlete. He started his company with just two shoes: one forward motion (running) and one lateral motion (tennis and basketball, etc). On one trip to the L.A. Merchandise Mart, I noticed a lonely man with only a card table set up in the booth. Most sales people had hundreds of samples and nice displays; some had decorated permanent rooms. I had read about this University of Oregon runner's new venture in an industry journal. Perhaps that is why I stopped to chat.

I felt sorry for him. Just two shoes. I picked up one of the shoes. He said, "Those are case goods." That is industry vernacular for products that came directly off the manufacturing line instead of being the hand built samples typically shown at a buyers' show. "Do you think you could sell those at $11.50?" This was a wholesale price. I quickly calculated that they could retail for $24.00 and still be two dollars cheaper than the top brand (Adidas) we were selling. The mark-up on Adidas was not what we called "key stone," or double the cost.

So Phil had me interested. Then he mentioned the bomb shell. 'Can you sell these if they are from South Korea?' Shoes made in Korea were still known to be of very inferior quality so I was skeptical. But I did buy both shoes to test. They sold fine, and Phil called me himself to get reorders.

We soon dropped athletic shoes, as the category was not really our niche, and it was becoming its own category (partially due to Phil Knight). We focused on leather goods, and clothing. Later I opened a little leather factory with friend Bill Rollin, to make completely unique goods so that we could control the distribution.

I bought out my retail mentors a few years later, because my ambition was to grow fast - faster than Don, Sr. would have been comfortable with. I was young and stupid and expected mistakes as we grew. Don Jr. and Don Sr. would not have been comfortable opening lots of stores, and I never wanted to stress my relationship with either of them. My new partner was David Boyd. We opened more stores together and started a leather and sportswear shop called Burgess Boyd. (I always thought that name had a nice ring!) Eventually we opened seven stores, each with a different theme.

During the early years, in the late 1960s, I saw Boot Hill, in Boulder, transform from a run-of-the-mill shoe store, to an exciting fashion leader. Just as students found new ways to express themselves, Don searched for products to allow that expression. Bell-bottom jeans, T-shirts, and blue work shirts were standard uniforms, so fashion expression was primarily focused on shoes, boots, sandals, leather vests and handbags and, of course, belts with large brass buckles. So, while seemingly impossible today, footwear stores led the fashion trends for several years among college students, and shaped the classic "hippie" look.

This hippie trend was completely foreign to the run-of-the-mill specialty shops, and especially to department stores. With layers of merchandise managers, and no department stores located where the action was (college campuses), they were blindsided. It is fair to say that they had absolutely no idea what was going on with the youth-oriented trends for a full decade. Moreover, the more conventional stores lost the college age kids as they aged over the next decade, and then lost those who were in high school, then junior high. So "baby boomers" and their increasing buying power (an emerging market) left department stores in droves.

Our initial market included college women; high school girls naturally followed. They were the powerhouse of fashion in those days, the ones who stated quite firmly that they would not be caught dead in a department store. We knew we had grabbed a market that was invisible to the department and chain stores. We had developed *our own crack in the market*, although I did not fully appreciate what that would mean for many years.

Being on the cutting edge often gets bloody. Eventually it would be bloody for us as well. But as a young man who had the hottest counter-culture designers (such as Bort Carlton, Dave Blakemore, Kenny Cole (the Kenneth Cole Company today) from the U.S. and Europe coming into the store to get advice (and sell some product too), it no doubt made us think we were really smart. We thought we were creating the market, but really we just understood it. The great movers and shakers of the time, wanted to see how we were dealing with the market, and what we were selling, not to get sage advice from us. While we were at ground zero with our market, we also thought it would last forever. We did have a strong run. During that 10 to 12 year period, we saw athletic shoes become standard street wear; hiking boots became standard footwear and, like 4X4 vehicles today, those boots almost never saw the mountains. We ushered in walking shoes and we sold so many Frye boots that lines of customers went down the street whenever we received a new shipment.

Our customers did not want to buy from the "establishment," so they sought out stores that were positioned to be *unlike* the other stores. We knew it was important to be different, so Don and I went up above Boulder, where he lived, and retrieved old mining timbers from some gold claims he still owned. We stained old (real) barn wood green so it looked like it had lichen on it. We used shake shingles, and found objects like old wooden boxes, dairy milk cans, battered tables with cracked paint, and stained glass windows. We put the 8" by 10" mine beams across the ceiling, and used the found objects as displays, on shelves and in the windows, to create "atmosphere." They were really cheap in those days. Today we call them "shabby chic" antiques.

When people walked through the door, they were hit with a complete sensual experience with the smell of old wood, leather and a few candles lit for good measure. It was completely unlike what anyone had experienced (unless they happened to live on an old farm in the mountains). Our success was immediately affirmed. Every day we heard "totally cool man" comments and watched facial expressions of amazement. No large store had the guts to try something like this. Across the country, however, small shops duplicated the look within a couple of years. We did not really invent it anyway. But we did produce the Colorado interpretation, which became a whole life style that John Denver and others later embraced.

The movement was so deep and universal that many communities spontaneously saw this new "crack" open at the same time. Many campuses, as well as shopping areas or other areas where folks in this market hung out—areas like Haight-Ashbury, Georgetown, Aspen, Westwood—-became even bigger magnets for the same. Boot Hill, and later our stores Old Soft Shoe and Burgess Boyd, were carefully positioned as "different"—-cool and hip. We competed with other similar stores in our own market area, but they were rare. In the Boulder market only one other shoe store could compete. And that store, was years behind. In the Denver market, Poor Richards, owned by the Chalfont's in the historic area of Larimer Square, competed with our four stores in different locations. That said, I must add that Poor Richards was one of the really fabulous leather shops in the nation. As we did so much business in boots, they eventually went into footwear as well, and were very respected merchants for many years. Located in a historic 1870s building, they were excellent at interior design and leather merchandising. I always envied their operation.

Therefore, with few competitors, those of us who were positioned for this crack all prospered. I'm sure we all thought we were just plain smart. But, in fashion all things change. By the mid-1970s things were changing fast. First disco swept the nation. Then the preppy look re-appeared. We, of course, adjusted, but by then, those of us who were fashion forward were being carefully watched by the chain and department stores. In the late '70s I surveyed a shopping mall where the *entire mall* had only two or three of the same SKU's, or stock-keeping units (styles). The next year it reversed. We only had three SKU's that were NOT in the mall. We saw our crack disappear even as we more quickly adapted to the styles, not knowing that we landed in another crack — one that traditional chains well understood.

Re-living these old experiences, I now realize that our crack had completely changed. It was like an earthquake. Because when leisure suits and then disco re-focused our customers on clothing *per se*, footwear again became "merely" an accessory. It no longer led the fashion trends for the baby boomers. Our crack in the market was displaced by another parallel crack, and that crack had moved back to the traditional footwear model. We did make the transition, but it was never the same. Growth slowed, business was not as exciting. We learned how to control inventory and manage costs, but the killer issue was more and more elusive. All the stores in our markets understood this old model. They merely had to buy what we bought, and the sales reps were all too happy to help them understand our buys.

Now I was learning what it was like to be in the same crack with many others. It is just brutal.

The final straw came in New York at the Plaza Hotel. Each company rented rooms, as temporary show rooms, on the same floor. The halls were crammed with buyers. I noticed that two young men were lurking at the open door in the hallway. I was the only one in the room with the sales representative, an old friend. I don't know why, but I asked him who they were. "Really?" he said. "You don't know that those guys are from Fashion Bar?" "No," I replied. "Well, their job is to watch every buy you make and then they place the order!"

I had been followed and courted for years, but never by a traditional fashion chain. Fashion Bar directly competed with me in two malls: one store was across the hall and another was just next door. Fashion Bar was moving heavily into footwear, and simply copying everything we did.

I felt the blood fall to my knees. Not an openly emotional person, I have rarely been so surprised by anything. I turned around again and they were gone. My friend the rep said, "They'll be back to get a copy of your detail sheets." "And you'll give it to them?" I asked in horror. "No, but most reps will. They are out for you. Be careful." I finished the show picking up every dog (meaning very ugly shoe) I saw. Reps looked at me like I had lost my mind, that is, totally lost my style-picking ability.

Keeping your head down in retail is very difficult, but this is even more difficult when every move is known months beforehand. I learned just how tough it could be competing with the big boys. They bought the same items we bought, and with their financial resources, they could bring in test samples much earlier than we could. They would spread a small order across many more stores than we could, so they had early test periods to reorder before we could afford to bring in the merchandise the first time.

Then, when we received the new shipment, they put those same items on sale, so we had to drop our price. As store designs changed and got updated, they could keep current with us, after having before taken years to catch up. The new crack we now played in was more like a valley, with lots of stores competing with each other. We had no place to hide. With one store, we might have retrenched and been able to survive. But two partners could not make a nice living in one store. As it was, we were too big to specialize by retreating to a former crack, and the new valley was too big for us to dominate.

At the time, we thought the great recession of 1980 was the primary challenge. Now looking back, we simply occupied the wrong crack. We had two new stores in a community that practically shut down early in the recession. Construction was the driving economic factor, and it just stopped in the same way it did again in 2008. The cost of closing those two stores was huge, but at least we remained in business with our original stores.

During this contraction of the early 1980s, fortunately an opportunity opened up for me in consulting. It was a perfect way to solve the salary problem of a smaller operation with two owners. After I left, the business languished and contracted for three more years. The recession was a huge problem, but the real problem was that our crack no longer existed. Financially weakened, the company finally faded away with just a whimper. Today, David Boyd and I remind ourselves of how we prospered in a very tough market. We agree that we learned more about how small business really works than either of us learned in business school. We both have re-built new businesses with cracks of our own. Business changes, but the one element—-"a crack of your own"—-we certainly understand better.

My consulting career was a refreshing change. I worked with other clothing retailers to plan their merchandise mix. The fashion retail industry is unique in its need to manage several seasonal buys per year. Called merchandise planning, this involves a very sophisticated mathematical model that looks at trends, markdowns, and supply and demand for catagories of merchandise and what is on-order, to calculate the correct "open-to-buy" on a continual basis. I understood this and the new computer inventory planning that went with it. My job was to sell planning services and to consult with stores in the Midwest. The computer was lowering the cost of developing these merchandising plans so that smaller specialty stores and independent department stores could afford the services and consulting that went with the reports.

In the 1980s the independent family stores in small towns were being threatened by Wal-Mart. The economy pushed many stores over the edge, but everyone blamed Wal-Mart. In town after town we saw empty storefronts.

While Wal-Mart did not steal every crack in the market, it did change traffic patterns in small towns where, on a regular basis, a new shopping center was built around the new Wal-Mart on cheaper land outside of town. This was a real problem for the existing small stores, which almost inevitably saw reduced traffic and therefore a significant drop in sales on items also sold by Wal-Mart. Remaining vital meant each store had to re-define its crack in the market. All the locally owned stores needed loyal customers who would come downtown specifically to shop at the few remaining stores.

For women's, men's and teen fashion stores, this was less of a problem; Wal-Mart has never captured much of the higher quality fashion market. However, the hardware, toy and home furniture markets were difficult to compete with. Some did make it: many did not. Those who did, transformed themselves into much deeper specialty stores. Deeper means they narrowed their categories of merchandise selection but bought deeper—more broadly—in sizes, colors and selections, or SKU's, again, the numbers assigned to each specific merchandise type, or stock-keeping units, for inventory control.

This kind of specialization is still an effective strategy for competing with Wal-Mart, because they concentrate on the higher volume areas of each department, and offer little variety, within one product, to select from. Customers can pick from one or two items at Wal-Mart for the benefit of a low price, but they don't expect much choice. Wal-Mart offers breadth of selection, but not depth within a product type. Many people shop for everyday basics at Wal-Mart, and go elsewhere if they don't find what they want. It works for Wal-Mart, because price-minded shoppers across the world may try Wal-Mart first. Today, Wal-Mart practically monopolizes the rather large valley in the general merchandise price market.

Competitors must pick their cracks carefully, choosing ones in which they can maneuver profitably. Many independent stores are now out of business, but not directly because of Wal-Mart. Their former competitors, the ones who specialized and deepened selection, could grow. They had to, because Wal-Mart existed. Sporting goods, furniture, pet shops, home improvement stores and others are all outcomes of competing in a market that demanded discovering a further crack in the market. "Big box" retailers in each category exist today where they previously did not.

Let's examine one industry in particular — the home improvement and building materials retailers. This category is now dominated by just a few players: By far the biggest is Home Depot, which was founded in 1978 and now has well over 2,200 stores, having branched out to every state in the country, all the territories, as well as Canada, Mexico, and China. Founded in 1946, Lowe's has over 1,750 stores in the United States, Australia, Canada, and Mexico. Where even the smallest towns used to have a lumberyard, most do not today.

Survivors found a differentiator to redefine their market niche. Today, specialty window and door shops still exist. They carry much more variety and provide complete services that the big boys just can't seem to coordinate so well. Other niche markets include stores like Restoration Hardware, custom cabinet shops, garage door installers, and deeply specialized fastener suppliers, and lamp specialty stores.

RMSA, the retail consulting company I worked for, had a great niche of its own. Retailers with seasonal or cyclical inventories have a difficult bookkeeping requirement. They must buy product for each season, and sell it before the season is over to avoid huge mark-downs. Fashion cycles also change but more slowly, as a new fashion gets started Recognizing this new trend means buyers must not overreact, based on the probability of full price sales, compared to throwing the excess away. It is a classic statistical probability problem. Only a few kinds of businesses have to deal with seasonal AND cyclical obsolescence. This calculation is commonly called "open-to-buy."

Calculating the proper inventory levels and this open-to-buy was quite laborious. Vernon Rossi founded his consulting company in 1953 to help small retailers improve their operations and profitability. At the time, over half of new retail stores failed in their first year; less than 5 percent were still in business three years later. Rossi teamed up with an early computer programmer and developed a computer model to provide those calculations. Indeed, in the 70s his company was renamed RMSA with the "A" standing for automation. RMSA created a unique id "ticket" for every piece of merchandise sold by its clients, and collected the data in order to generated sales reports.

Suddenly a market was born where experienced merchandisers could use a computer-generated product with consultation to a retailer without doing all that laborious math. Other companies and retailers knew how to calculate open-to-buy, but adding the capacity of a computer and using seasonal data from other stores added much more power. This represents a classic case of combining a traditional management accounting practice with technology, to create a new product. RMSA was then able to hire and train consultants to deliver these services all over the country.

The budgeting problem solved, and the in-house technology at hand, the individual unit or SKU inventory problem could be tackled. I won't delve too much into the inventory management weeds here, but in the late 1970s computing power was just beginning to tackle huge data projects. Keeping track of dollars in a category was not memory intensive. But keeping track of a single item with the attributes of vendor, category, style, color, and size, for thousands of items was a huge problem. Managing inventory at this micro level (literally each unique object) required a unique blend of technology, specialized industry knowledge and an understanding of open-to-buy planning. A new crack was created. No competitors with open-to-buy planning software existed in the specialty fashion business, so the company grew rapidly from the mid 70s through the mid-80s.

Exploiting his understanding of soft goods retailing, and computers, Rossi developed an advanced inventory system that used "factors" for sell-through ratios, turnover, on-order and selling rates for each category and style across multiple stores.

These services were expensive. Each purchase order was sent to the company where they were keyed into the main frame computer. Then special price tags were printed for every item. Returned to the store, one part of the tag was removed when the item was received, another when it was sold, another if inventory was taken, and the last part stayed with the product in case it was returned.

Each tag had a cost and so only expensive items could be put on the system. This was generally called the "service bureau" business. Computers were rented based on use. While these services were expensive in the service bureau environment, many high-end and couture store clients bought the service.

By 1984, the huge business potential of personal computers was just beginning to be apparent. Re-writing the software to work on PC's seemed like a plausible way to eliminate the per-unit tag cost. The price of the service could be reduced and would become more economical for additional retailers.

The market was ripe for such an early entry into the inventory management system business. Relationships were already established. We already had over 2000 specialty stores as merchandise planning clients, and they all would eventually need an inventory system. As the industry leader RMSA was poised for a huge entry into what today is a mammoth market.

After two years of development, the PC software project was moved into the department I directed, Management Services. This essentially meant everything that didn't make money! As the project leader, I had the responsibility of completing the software product and launching the marketing for it.

We wrote and formatted manuals on brand new Macintosh computers, and I become competent on the new IBM 386. Because I was a former small retailer, and understood the personal computer, I knew my career was set. My inaugural sales trip took me to 10 merchandising planning clients in eight days. I closed five of them for $22,500 each, when expensive software for the PC seldom cost over $1000. In addition, each client would pay monthly transaction fees. We had discovered a bonanza. All I had to do was manage the installations.

But at this point Rossi stumbled badly. He listened to his young controller, who, being a bean counter, was more worried about short-term revenue loss than long-term success. Within weeks of my return, the un-imaginative controller, aided by one or two myopic managers, pulled the plug. They felt I would put the computerized inventory service bureau out of business. They made me refund deposit checks to cancel the orders. Two companies insisted that they would sue if we did not allow them the software. Many of us were, naturally, flabbergasted.

We had about three million dollars (back when a dollar was still a dollar) invested in a really good system. Undoubtedly I could sell hundreds or thousands of systems. Yet the other executives said I was going to erode the service bureau business on the mainframe. Service bureau was a business where customers paid us for each transaction we processed, an expensive and limited market. It was clear that a market existed and because we completely occupied the merchandise planning market crack, and had experience in inventory management, we had the chance to displace NCR, with modern PC cash register systems. We had stumbled into an emerging crack in the market, and had the resources to fill it.

It only took a few years for the competition to catch up (although with inferior systems). In any case, it was the *competitors* who made the service bureau obsolete. So with much of the revenue eroded, management chose to invest another million dollars to explore a new system. Well, by then, it was a failing company. One hundred and twenty field consultants were completely demoralized and the company dropped to half the number of field consultants after a buyout.

As brilliant as Rossi was in some ways, he was uneducated outside of his life's work. Meanwhile, other top people were completely unaware of the new crack in the market that technology created for the company. When the new company president eventually acknowledged the horrible mistake, it was much too late. Of course, the retail computer cash register and inventory market is now in the billions of dollars.

I should point out that, for various reasons, the people who were involved in this decision are like most small business people. They missed the boat exactly like millions who have missed the boat. In a sense, they cannot be blamed. They were all intelligent folks; they just didn't understand how to move from one crack to an adjacent crack. The vast majority of business people make the same mistake. Even now, their exclusive merchandise planning crack is heavily challenged by former field consultants who saw room in the same crack. Today RMSA is a mere shadow of itself, having once been the envy of this little niche market.

I soon realized that, with the new inventory software crack gone, I too needed a new one. A few of us saw the vulnerability of the old company in areas that management failed to pick up on. One module I wanted to add at RMSA was a customer tracking function, so we could keep track of who bought what and then promote directly to their tastes. This seems like a good idea now, don't you think? But this was never to enjoy even a serious discussion. Today tracking customers and customer management systems (CRM's) are also a multi-billion dollar market!

I left RMSA within a month of the decision to drop the PC software. I expected to continue consulting in the retail market, with an emphasis on what I knew about customers and marketing. Instead, I started thinking about how difficult it was for small businesses to market to small groups of people. One exception is direct mail. But to use direct mail to maximum effect, one needs customer addresses, as well as a way to classify their interests or buying behaviors. Following customer buying habits was similar to communicating with only those in your crack in the market. Moreover, it was a way to compete with large companies that could afford the mass media of newspapers, radio and TV. Within a year, I was working with businesses outside the retail industry. In five years, I had far fewer retail clients than other types of businesses such as industrial and fabricating companies, business services, wholesale and agribusiness.

I had a wonderful time at RMSA, and was privileged to work with many smart business consultants. Twenty years later, I still keep in touch with some of them. I miss the old company. One project I enjoyed was gathering hundreds of clients' financial statements in order to load expenses into a database for analysis. We developed a little product that would help retailers identify costs—and thereby lower them. We loaded all kinds of additional information into the database: location type, city and neighborhood type, ownership type, and of course merchandising information such as markdowns, margins and sales. It was a bomb: No one really wanted someone else to plan their expenses. But the information and knowledge I gained was enormous.

This was probably the first glimmer of my understanding that retail success had a lot to do with location types. We discovered that many stores in cities with percentage rent leases would never make much money. This was because of the mix of variable expenses to fixed expenses. In those days, selling costs were about 15 percent, advertising about 3 percent and another 7 percent was for rent above a base rent. Therefore, every dollar carried *forever* an astounding cost of 25 percent. The merchandise can cost from 55 to 65 percent after markdowns, so the variable cost is now at over 75 percent. The business still needed to pay for fixed expenses (those costs that will go on even if the door never opens). It takes lots of quarters (what is left after the 75 percent) to pay for other fixed costs.

I had clients who were leasing in high profile locations, where the costs to construct the tenant improvements were so high that they would never have enough quarters to pay for them. Compare this scenario with small family stores in small towns where my clients owned their building outright. In these cases, a limited amount of advertising was sufficient, because everyone knew them already. They worked hard at buying right, so they could cover markdowns, and ended up with a 12 to 15 percent net profit! They did not look as slick as the high profile shops. But they filled their own market crack and made far more money than the high profile stores in up-scale malls.

Discovering this principle, I began to focus on why some businesses are so successful, while other ones, whose owners and managers do so much that is right, at least according to business schools, just don't make it. *Why do business people who become rich, actually make it?* Answering this question has been my quest ever since.

Over the decades of developing my practice, I have seen that the difficulty of a business has much to do with what crack it is trying to fill. In all cases, the owners need a certain level of competency in the service or in buying products. However, the level of success also is closely connected with how many others are in the same crack.

Marketing is the process of matching a company's competency with customer needs or wants. But this process is successful or disrupted by the number of competitors in the same crack. This adds a "lucky" component to almost every successful business.

As someone who has carefully observed many different types of businesses and customers, and who has many years of experience in niche marketing, I have come to understand "Finding Your Own Crack In Your Market."

I am gratified that my long-time clients have all grown, from 100 percent to 1000 percent. In many ways, it's not that I am a better "marketer" or better at marketing promotion. It's because, over the years, I have carefully charted a course for leadership in a market niche, a crack in the market. Now that you understand where I'm coming from, you should be able to see how your business can benefit from this explanation of my experiences.

I have never forgotten these axioms:

If a company or product is uniquely positioned in a market with ample demand, the rest of what gets lumped under the marketing umbrella can be skipped.

Marketing is a complete discipline designed to compensate for the lack of proper market emplacement.

Don Griffith said, "If people want what you have they will beat a path to your door."

So how do you create products and services that customers want, in a niche of your own? I call this process *market emplacement*. This book was written to discuss the principles of Marketing Emplacement to give small business owners a better understanding of how building a business that creates wealth is achieved.

Chapter 1 Introduction

The small business landscape is wide and diverse. It is wide in the sense that it embraces many thousands of small niche businesses that evolve and adapt to the marketplace. It is diverse in that it includes all types of people, from all backgrounds.

Yet, only some people have what is required to succeed in a small business. Some are simply not cut out to take risks and work untold hours. Others may be successful in the first stages, but cannot go on to become effective managers. Chapter 8, "What does the successful business person look like?" will elaborate on this issue of what kinds of people are most likely to succeed in business. Meanwhile, let's just say for now that success is not a matter of intelligence. While intelligence is helpful in business, people without high IQs can succeed. Very intelligent people can fail. The reason is that finding your crack in the market is more important.

Put in another way, my three decades of business consulting shows that hard-working people of entirely average intelligence can make a nice living simply by providing good service in a crack in the market. They

43

can succeed because they are where no one else is. Perhaps they have little or no competition because of their geographic location. Or perhaps it's the extreme specialty of their offerings, or the development of a mutually beneficial relationship with another referral business.

> Joe rebuilds engines. He's pretty good at it. All his business comes from his brother-in-law, who has a very successful auto shop. Joe gets all of his brother-in-law's business. So, as his brother-in-law prospers, Joe's business increases.

The symbiotic relationship works because Joe provides a service to a market without competition, and his brother-in-law needs a reliable vendor for services he does not provide, and now does not need to provide. America—-indeed, the world—-has millions of such examples.

Niches

Geography still creates small markets—despite the Internet. On vast expanses of near-empty highways in the U.S. west, dozens of businesses cater to travelers. Tow trucks can only be effective along a limited number of miles. In many areas one tow truck company services a stretch of more than 100 miles, covering perhaps three very small towns. Unlike the restaurant and lodging industries, the nature of the towing business makes it tough for national companies to gain a foothold in isolated local communities. Geography creates cracks in the market for hundreds of services, from plumbers, to doctors and hospitals, to retailers and insurance agents.

Very small niche markets can also exist across large geographic areas, but operate in small cracks in the market because of narrow specialties. These niches exist all around us. Some are obscure and unimportant. Others are essential to maintaining the national standard of living. Either way, most of us never think about them; even the crucial ones never register to a typical consumer.

Take the example of large industrial motors. These literally maintain today's standard of living by pumping water, operating manufacturing plants, crushing rock, running commercial buildings' air conditioning, lifting elevators and many other critical functions. But when these large motors break down, because of their age or special function, repairing them is much more cost effective than buying a new motor. Because large motors are heavy, shipping charges create regional markets for motor repair shops. Rewinding the burned out motor wire is a specialized trade; it requires experience and a high level of electrical knowledge.

So when modern electrical power stations and transmission were invented in 1893,[1] a new niche business emerged to repair the large motors and generators. At first, the engineers themselves had to repair them. But as more and more power systems were built and motors made other power sources obsolete, the market grew to a specialty. That new niche business meant engineers no longer had to spend their time doing repair work. And the niche still continues.

Motors are absolutely essential to the modern economy, so we will have motor repair facilities for at least hundreds of years. However, more recently, motors have become more sophisticated, so a new niche has developed to deal with the premium efficiency motors and computer electronics required to run them. The motor shops that could not keep up with the level of sophistication are slowly dying. Those who have made the transformation, however, are filling the crack in the market.

Each type of crack (niche, geographic, symbiotic, technological, and others) gets filled by those who recognize the market or have a skill or interest in the product or service. Those people come from all backgrounds and include smart and average people, all races and creeds, and varied personalities. But their success in filling those cracks depends on both *vision* and *luck*. That is, businesses very rarely succeed entirely on the basis of vision.

If you throw enough mud on the wall, some of it will stick

Why can people who are essentially "average" succeed in this competitive world? Because, they are not in competitive markets. They are filling their own cracks in the market. Recognizing the crack is the key to long term success, although by no means is success guaranteed. We tend to remember only the survivors. Even with the survivors, we tend not to hear about their earlier failures. Nonetheless, the businesses we see today are the result of many more trials, including ones that failed in one way or another, competing in many small battles for small niche markets. The old term "If you throw enough mud on the wall, some of it will stick," describes the reality of the 90 percent of businesses that could not stick. Many people fail because they are undercapitalized or cannot manage money. Others cannot hire or keep people. Some like the independence of owning their own business, but lack the discipline or sacrifice to keep with it.

My 40 years of observing and analyzing small business suggests that even people with the talents mentioned above can still fail. Perhaps they selected a market where no market existed. Perhaps the cracks were already filled. Smart business school graduates fail in business all the time, too. They have business skills, learned how to manage cash flow and read financial statements. Most even try to assess the market and pick winners, but they still fail. Even seasoned business people who start additional businesses in their area of expertise fail, because they launched yet another competitor in an already crowded market.

The remainder of this book explores these realities in more depth. The goal is to help you use extreme care in selecting a crack. And for those of you already in business, this will help you fight for your crack while finding ways to grow into new ones or enlarge your crack to succeed in a larger market.

Chapter 2   What is small business and why does it matter?

The spectrum of business size between small and large is about as wide as one could imagine today. The difference between General Electric and your local electrician is obvious. The differences between a 100 employee electric service company and a 5000 employee corporation are less obvious. And, while it is currently in vogue to celebrate smaller businesses while "Wall Street" and the Mega Corporation are demonized, the gradual size increases and the corresponding changes in behavior and motivations are poorly understood.

In my mind, the **single person proprietorship** is an entirely different organization than one with a payroll that must consistently be met. The single person proprietorship includes those who are transitioning from another job to start up a business, as well as those who are full time tradesmen and professionals who have managed to create a job for themselves. But when a single person proprietorship (even if it is incorporated), hires its next full time producing employee, it becomes a micro-business. Making that first payroll changes the owner's mindset and the way the business must operate to insure payroll is unfailingly paid.

Proprietorship

Since a single person proprietorship primarily sells one person's services, the revenue limitation is based on how much one person alone can produce. This limitation essentially remains even if they have part-time or even full time help, whether in the office or an employee who is unskilled in the trade.

A single person proprietorship can do very well. Some manage to create revenue of the several hundred thousand dollars. But for the vast majority, the revenue is within the general range of working for another company, once all expenses are paid. Meanwhile, they work much longer hours and are always "on-call." Besides doing the work, the lone proprietors must find the work and account for the work. Rarely do they get rich. When they retire, they can occasionally sell their "book" of work. Nonetheless, that amounts to a great bonus, not a retirement pension, because the work itself directly depended on the individual. When they are gone, the value goes with them.

Why might these people actually do this, one may rightly ask? Obviously, some are otherwise unemployed. Others begin their own businesses because they want the independence that comes with working for oneself. They get to do things the way they believe in. While on the whole they put in many more hours than an employee ever would, they believe they have flexibility. They are the living symbol of the eighteenth century American Individualist that De Tocqueville celebrated. These folks are confident of their skills and their ability to do everything that needs to be done. Most businesses are started for just a few important reasons: owners want autonomy and independence; they want a better income; or they have a passion to succeed in business. Finally they see a void in the marketplace or a problem that they can solve and have an innate drive to do so. And if they fail, they will be better workers for another company for having witnessed first-hand the difficulties of working alone. Most never get to the point of making that first full time hire. But many dream of it.

The crack in the market that they operate in is by necessity largely created slowly, by creating relationships, and those relationships create referrals that are turned into relationships. In the past they were very local, but in the last decade many people have been able to use the Internet and technology to extend their geographic reach. Even so, for the most part, they still operate in a relationship niche and a technical niche.

Micro-businesses

Given the advantages of technology, automation, and computers, one person can successfully operate a micro-business. As long as the person is selling the products or services, administrative staffers are not always necessary. Micro-businesses that effectively sell other services or products can acquire all the systems necessary for larger businesses, such as sophisticated invoicing systems, marketing and communications, professional websites, and a selling network or distribution system.

People who intend to start their own business sometimes acquire specific skills in order to occupy the niche they have identified. But generally they already have a business orientation (rather than a blue collar trade orientation or a white collar profession). They hope to soon be able to hire that first helper, and shortly after the first, second and third employee. They intend to be successful enough to do so. The single person proprietorship is content with doing well while practicing their particular skill, even if they do eventually make the jump to the micro-business. For the single person proprietorship, making a good living is success. For the micro-business, in contrast, hiring is success. Both, however, love the challenge, independence and responsibility.

Small Business

Once a small micro-business hires three or four people, it becomes a small business. Most never make it to this size. But those who do must then demonstrate enough leadership to manage or direct these people in a productive way. This is big step for many businesses. Understanding cash management is critical as well; for businesses over five years old, growth and lack of cash is often what kills them, not the lack of a good niche market. If they lack excellent cash management skills (and this is much harder than most people think), then being very conservative with cash and growth can keep them in business simply because they are misers and scared to miss a payment.

When employment is around 12 to 20 people, depending on the industry, the level of management sophistication changes. Employee benefits, cash flow, marketing, accounting and taxes, and managing a dozen or more people create new challenges. Good managers can solve these issues by hiring professionals. Others with the intellect and drive may insist on doing these added tasks themselves.

Medium Sized Small Businesses

For purposes of this discussion, let's call organizations with 20 to 100 employees the "medium sized small businesses." Those with 100 to 250 employees are the "large small businesses." Businesses with over 250 employees often experience the same problems as the very large corporations. Running a company with over 100 employees generally must be done differently than when it was small: the division of labor, supervision, and branching into new businesses that get out of control all require a different philosophy. Most of these larger businesses have transitioned to much stronger business managers with different skill sets.

Most people think that the SBA defines a small business as having fewer than 500 employees. This is not true. The SBA's criteria are that it is independently owned and operated, is organized for profit, and is not dominant in its field. The size standard or sales volume figure depends on the industry. In retailing, for example, according to the SBA, annual receipts may not exceed $5 million to $21 million, depending on the particular product.

When categorizing businesses by number of employees, as the SBA acknowledges, it's important to recognize that some industries are more labor intensive than others. For instance, a manufacturing company with 50 employees will have much larger revenue than a service organization with the same number of employees. Perhaps the factory has three people in the office and 47 low paid workers on the line. The manufacturer will still be very small with 50 employees. Meanwhile a service organization with 50 is very respectable; it may be very sophisticated with several highly paid managers.

The most significant division between smaller and huge companies may come when the ownership changes from a few individuals to lots of stockholders. When the one, two or three founders of a company are still in control, the company still operates like a paternal (or, more so lately, maternal) dictatorship. When one company is owned by another, or it is a public stock company, the entire emphasis turns to profit and return on investment.

Return on Investment

Those of you already part of large companies or formally educated in business, are saying, "What? Isn't return on investment what all business is about?" The answer is a clear and emphatic, "NO."

Years ago, when I was working for a small non-profit, the C.S. Lewis Foundation, I attended a regional conference in Los Angles attended mostly by Christian educators. Perhaps naturally, I attended the business breakout, where the discussion quickly turned to business ethics. The conversation centered around "shady" industries where individuals found it difficult to maintain ethics and still get the deal done. A fairly prosperous physician, who owned a very successful dialysis clinic, raised several questions about the purpose of business and why ethics were critical for Christians. He wondered what business schools taught

54

students concerning ethics. The two business professors (one from Pepperdine and one from a state university) who were moderating the discussion said that some ethics were taught but that the goal of a business school was to teach the management principles that lead to maximizing return on investment (how much can a business earn based on how much was invested in the business).

Several small business people attending this meeting expressed shock, especially because it was a Christian forum. My physician friend stated that he never considered return on investment. This claim received looks of dismay from both professors. (They did not know just how wealthy my friend had become in his dialysis business.) Finally I had to stop the group and explain to the professors why their assumptions about large business did not apply to small ones: "After 20 years of working for hundreds of small businesses, I have never, even once, had the owner ask me to increase their Return on Investment, let alone maximize it!" At this fairly simple statement, the small business people in the room nodded their complete understanding. The professors looked perplexed. The notion that the purpose could be anything else was out of their grasp.

Small businesses are very rarely launched to maximize the owner's return on investment. With their very high publicity profile, today's tech startups may make it seem the case; but these involve folks trying to start a big business, not a small one. They too must find a crack in the market to grow and prosper, but they do so with the intent of creating a valuable company to eventually sell.

This is not the case with 99 percent of new small businesses, whose entrepreneurs imagine a successful business that can generate a comfortable income. Perhaps some of them dream that it will become valuable enough to sell at a nice profit, even make them rich. But people who try to calculate ROI do so because they think this is what business people do.

ROI is for investors. Understanding the relative return for an investment compared with another set of investments is useful for decision making. It is a classic business measure. Before I understood what I now know, I even showed clients how to calculate it! Now I understand why they were only moderately interested.

When a small business is still small, it pours all its resources into growth, investment, and people to produce the products and services to support the growth. It is only when the growth slows and when, having paid off much of its debt, the business throws off cash that can be used for additional, optional investment. When that finally happens, understanding the ROI forecast becomes as important for decision making as for the investor who weighs the risk of losing the money with the percentage return of the investment. Most small business owners in this situation begin to look at yields as any other investor might. But if a new machine is needed, the evaluation is more likely "can we make the payments" than what will the ROI be. They either know they need the machine, or want it. And if the owner wants it, and can pay for it, he buys it. This is exactly why they wanted to be in business: to have control of it.

So the differences in motivations between small and large corporations are substantial. The small company that acts like a large company is the anomaly. Even in that rare case, it's because the owner <u>chooses</u> to run it that way, not that it <u>must</u> be that way.

Big Business

Publicly traded stock companies have been around just over 400 years. Prior to that, all business was accomplished by those who owned the business outright.

Very large expeditions, such as war or exploration of faraway places, required very large investments. Only royal families could afford such costs. Every American school child knows that the exploration of Christopher Columbus was financed by the Spanish Queen Isabella and her husband King Ferdinand. They were able to provide the funding because they had unburdened their kingdom of the huge debt Isabella's brother had incurred. (What is less known is that Columbus got half of his financing from private Italian investors, and he had to lobby and negotiate with the royals for a couple of years.) The discovery of the new world, and the subsequent "development" of central and south America, not only made Spain a major power but also made clear to many Europeans that trade with faraway places could be very profitable for them as well.

The English and the Dutch were the first to think about formal ways to share the risk of these huge investments. The East India Company was launched by London businessmen who banded together in 1600 to import spices from South Asia. With their superior navigational technology and skills, the Spanish and Portuguese had monopolized the East Indies spice trade. But destruction of the Spanish Armada in 1588 allowed the British and Dutch to enter this highly profitable import business. With a license from the British Parliament (officially revoked in 1813), the East India Company could exploit a huge trade monopoly—in its niche. No single business owner could risk the lost ships and cargo. The Company therefore sold stock. For a share of the investment, a person could get a share of the profits; and profits were huge given the monopoly on hundreds of highly valued and desired goods (not just spices but also indigo, silk, and cotton) from the Far East. Many in the upper classes were given the privilege of purchasing stock, and became wealthier as a result. The investment to equip many ships with the latest technology and sailors, for months at a time, as well as establishing a beachhead half way around the world, was similar to going the moon, some 300 years later.

Seven years later the same "joint-stock company" concept was used to finance another extraordinary venture, that of establishing Jamestown in Virginia. The East India Company was a boon, but the Virginia Company of London was a bust. The Virginia Company did succeed in establishing an English colony in the New World, but not in producing wealth for its shareholders. Management of the company proved to be difficult. Without a proprietor on site, new methods of command and control had to be set up. And unlike the Indies to the East, the "Indians" to the west were less than enthusiastic about the new town. Communications were months old before managers could react.

Jamestown was a disaster for the two thirds of settlers who lost their lives over its first three years. Moreover, it was one of the first corporate disasters in history. For the first time, the people who owned the company were not the same people who ran the company. Of course most of the managers were invested in the Virginia Company, but they only lost their investment; they were not responsible for enormous debts racked up in the colony. In a vicious cycle, decision-making became self-serving and was fraught with political and class distinctions that applied little to financial success.

The first really big project in the United States involving public sale of stock was the building of the Union Pacific Railroad to California. The project required huge government support, in the way of cash and land, in order to make ownership seem palatable. We celebrate the golden spike as the completion of a huge move forward in transportation, connecting our expanding nation. And so it was. But the management and building of the railroad was turned into a huge pork barrel project as the incentives for completion were misplaced, the profitability questionable, and the financing slimy at best. Again, the ownership had been disengaged from the management and the purpose was largely political.

Over the years, the corporation as an entity has become much better managed. The first business schools were founded to teach young men how to maintain the value of large companies for their owners. Indeed only recently have business schools attempted to offer courses on "entrepreneurship," which remains a fuzzy relationship to small business. The properly run corporation creates as much security as possible to

59

bring more people to the market to buy its stock. It well knows that profits directly translate into returns for investors. Individual investors compare all forms of investment against risk to determine where to place their excess investment dollars. To manage the very large enterprise, modern management techniques have become extremely sophisticated. Armies of accountants, consultants and lawyers attempt to maintain control of systems, finance, and the profits that must be reported quarterly for the investment market. Today's large corporation must play the investment game to avoid a selloff of its stock for that quarter. Meanwhile, armies of PR folks and mortgage bankers spin the story to create a market. The modern corporation by necessity must act rationally.

The small business shares DNA with the large corporation, but it is normally a different species, with different motivations. Small business owners want to live a lifestyle different from corporate employees. Their definition of success is as much emotional as it is financial remuneration. Most will count success both ways, and, of course, desire financial security. But they do not regard their businesses as a precise investment on money invested.

Therefore, the techniques that small business owners use for decision making derive from a paradigm that certainly is not one driving the large corporation. Oddly, then, most business advisors, academics, and management consultants still try to convert big business strategy to small business strategy. It is possible, but only with extreme care and experience. Unfortunately, many of the prescriptions that solve the problems of big business are simply wrong for small business.

Chapter 3   Cracks

We are constantly aware of certain large markets: computer manufacturers, cell phones, automobiles, retail hard goods, and soft goods. All of these markets were once very small niche markets, as is quickly evident from a little historical review. And while the global economy evolved in much the same way, looking at the rapid development of the U.S. economy over four centuries gives us the complete cycle.

The first English development in America was as much an economic endeavor as a political one. As England gained naval power, it recognized that keeping its old enemy Spain at bay might be accomplished by settling the New World. In 1606, as the previous chapter mentioned, the planners and founders of the Virginia Company of London were "merchant adventurers." Certainly it was an adventure to discover new lands and people; but the merchants realized, based on extremely lucrative trading with the East India Company, that the "adventures" could be financed by new products not otherwise available, one that traded at high margins back home. And of course in those days, the world well understood the value of gold that was brought to Spain from Central and South America.

The cost of building ships, and supplying and manning these complex expeditions was enormous. The founders of the Virginia Company hoped above all that they would find gold and silver as the Spanish had. They were mistaken. After much strife and death and finally re-organization, the members of the colony in Jamestown, Virginia, realized that they must first support themselves, and create a tradable product if they were to survive long term.

Incidentally, both Jamestown and Plymouth first attempted communal farms. In Virginia, they all worked for the "Company." So there was little incentive to work any harder than what the whip demanded. In Plymouth, it was a "team" of like-minded people who wanted freedom. Neither type of incentive worked. They separately discovered that only working for oneself created the incentive to prosper. Once this incentive was released by the freedom to buy and keep land, the colonists slowly began to grow more crops than they needed to survive, creating cash crops. Then they found additional products that thrived.

The first new crack in the market in the New World was envisioned by John Rolfe. Tobacco was used throughout the Caribbean and the southeastern seaboard by Native Americans. But the local tobacco tasted harsh by European standards. Rolfe knew that tobacco was bought and used by Europeans; at some point he heard about, or was brought, cuttings of a milder type of tobacco thought to be from the Caribbean. He first cultivated experimental tobacco crops in the second township of the colony, Henrico City.[2] Setting his farm up just a mile or so away in Varina, he created his first crop for market in 1612.

The crack in the market? It was a milder form of tobacco that Europeans took to immediately. The fact that tobacco is highly addictive, probably not understood then, created a larger and larger market. Rolfe created the first export product and literally ensured the long term success of the Virginia colony. He personally prospered from the product while it was a small crack in the market. In fact it made Rolfe and his wife Pocahontas famous. But as demand pushed the price up, the crack rapidly widened. Many other "planters" began to develop tobacco as well. But Rolfe was an innovator, not a businessman, and the Virginia Company needed a cash crop. Had he been a businessman he would have attempted to patent his new formulation or dominate the market. As more and more farmers turned to tobacco, the price finally plummeted in the 1660s.[3] It was a simple case of supply and demand. Rolfe would not become wealthy. Another market leader would emerge.

The business visionaries of the time knew that they needed two things to prosper with tobacco in a big way: land and labor. To the extent they could, they reinvested in both. The new agribusiness men who could grow faster began to control the land next to deep water ports on the rivers, where they cultivated, aged and shipped the tobacco from one plantation. Land was bought, or acquired, through political means. Labor was attracted by paying for transportation from England to Virginia where the "indentured" paid back the cost of transportation by servitude.

Robert "King" Carter, for example, was a businessman who became phenomenally wealthy and powerful.[4] Farmers could no longer get rich on a few acres of tobacco. But Carter became politically connected with the Governor (and at one point was the acting Governor). As such Carter was able to legally acquire thousands of acres of land, in return for improving the land. He amassed enough capital to bring many indentured workers to Virginia and supplemented that labor force with African indentured servants who in 1680 became slaves. Carter was the Bill Gates of the seventeenth century: Knowing that efficiencies cut costs, he obtained many very large plantations. He hired tradesmen to build his own facilities including shipping docks, stores for trade, and manufacturing of various needed items. His plantations were completely self-sufficient. The Carter family maintained this huge business for generations. Fast forward to 1970 and find just a few huge tobacco companies controlling the industry. These few companies could reap high profits because they were an oligopoly: a few large companies controlling a whole market. At the same time, hundreds of small farmers barely eke out a living in a now huge market — a niche that had grown into a wide valley.

With goods to trade, many high grade manufactured goods were shipped back to America from England: silverware, china, fine furniture and clothing, wine and beer. It cost less to ship a cask across the Atlantic than to transport it 100 miles into the interior, so coastal communities became wealthier and the standard of living increased.

With a basic cash crop, Virginia and other colonies began to thrive, and as their population grew, pushing into the interior was necessary to find land to grow food, tobacco and later cotton. As the cattle industry grew, local leather was available. Boot making became a local trade instead of an import, as boots could be made cheaper and better where the foot could be measured and fitted in person.

This became true of many other trades, including iron smithing (tool making) and horseshoeing. Each of these trades required special knowledge and skills that most farmers lacked. Each settlement that grew up around farmers was a small niche, a crack in the market. Artisans filled these cracks as the towns and nation grew. As canals and railroads developed, each dropped the cost of shipping compared to mule teams or wagon shipment costs.

Enterprising boot makers realized that new cracks were now available to them in other towns if they could only reduce the cost of production. They did so by developing wooden lasts of uniform sizes to stretch the leather on. The work force was divided into specializations. Many years before Ford implemented the assembly line, there were people who cut, or sewed, or pulled lasts, or made soles. Given how specializations helped save time, and their additional leverage for buying materials, smaller shoe factories could lower their prices below the threshold of the shipping costs. Gradually they put the custom boot maker out of business. They filled the boot maker's crack in the market by beating his value proposition.

Similar markets were filled by the wagon makers, plow builders and other specialized tool makers, pushing the blacksmith into a smaller and smaller part of his original crack. In 1840, a blacksmith could easily set up business. All he needed were tools, a hearth in an old shed, and some skill. If enough farmers and small factories were nearby, business thrived. If too many blacksmiths were in town, someone moved or went back to farming. After railroads opened up access to most of the East by 1860, however, the best plow could be purchased across the country and easily and cheaply shipped anywhere. The best and most fashionable shoes could be made anywhere as well. The cost of custom made shoes was so high that manufactured shoes from the East could be shipped west and still be lower in cost. Following the Civil War, New England boot makers who had been turning out boots for soldiers in necessarily large quantity had excess capacity. This eventually displaced the local shoe and boot maker. But the makers of these goods needed a way to show their goods. First, traveling traders and their wagons filled the bill; later, retail general stores followed. New distribution cracks showed up to fill the opportunity. Retailers bought plows, boots and shoes, tools and confectionaries creating a consumer market niche. Each product and each distribution method created a crack to be filled. In turn, each new crack was filled mostly by tradesmen or by people who intentionally sought to discover a way to create and fill a crack. Many more tried and failed than succeeded for exactly the same reasons businesses fail today.

The railroad business and new steamboats put most of the engineless inland water transportation out of business. The small crack created at the outset of rail development in the 1840s grew into a huge enterprise with dozens of geographic markets in the country by the 1870s. Fast forwarding to the 1960s and we start to see massive disruption in a large market with consolidation of railroads and retailers. As the market became national, the geographic cracks vanished and became part of the bigger market. As the market began to shrink with air and truck transport, the larger players squeezed all the small players out of their old cracks. Now the entire rail industry has just a few players. Where hundreds of niche market railroads existed just 80 years ago, only a few remain today.

The retail business has inherent geographic cracks because most people buy within a certain time or distance limit from home. So as the country population grew denser after 1880, the retailers began to reap larger and larger markets. The cracks in each area (hardware, clothing, home furnishings, and appliances) all grew. Smaller successful retailers saw both prestige and economy of scale in larger "department" stores. Many millionaires were made in this era: Wanamaker, Marshall Field, May, Sears, and Penny are a just few. Marshall Field captured the middle and upper market. In contrast, J.C. Penny was conservative, keeping prices low, and requiring each sales person to turn in the spent pencil nub, before issuing a new one.

Every town typically had several independent retailers. Most were specialty stores such as hardware, clothing, druggists, butchers, bakers, furniture and appliances; but some were even more specialized. The general store was supplanted by the depth of the specialty store, which survived by offering new and different merchandise. Then the specialty store was beat by the convenience and scale of the department store. Now the department store is bitterly battling the discount store and the broad based, big box discount specialty store.

As towns grew, the competition got stiffer, and the profit margins smaller. Today the retail industry as a whole has squeezed profits to the minimum, because so many players are still fighting for the large markets that are now national and global with Internet buying. The industry calls this "over-retailed." While we still have thousands of retail stores, the bulk of business is done by a few large chains like Costco, Federated, and of course Wal-Mart and Sam's Club. Many smaller family stores went out of business as the large chains continue to expand from city to suburb to other towns and states. These very large operations enjoy such sheer buying power and distribution that they keep new entries out. No individual thinks, "Let's open up a national chain of discount stores!" Only the already large retailers have the resources to think that way. Most of the second tier retailers are just happy to stay in the black, a goal made more difficult in tough economic times.

Transportation and communication costs were the tools needed for the retail business to be so greatly transformed in the twentieth century. West Coast factories could now sell to East Coast retailers. So, nearly all product market cracks have been transformed from small geographic markets into very large national markets. No room exists now for inferior products, because all products in each crack compete with all other products. As this happens, only a few survive, because people want to buy the most *valuable* product.

History shows us that the natural transformation of markets is no different than it is today. New products arise due to a unique breed of innovators. Most fail, but some markets grow and prosper. They usually start out as very tiny cracks in the market. A very few grow into large markets, where they become filled with competitors who eventually consolidate or drive each other out of business due to heavy competition. This consolidation many times leads to an oligopoly (a few large competitors in large markets), who continue to prosper until a new competing innovation disrupts the old market.

From Rolfe's tobacco to today's Internet companies, innovating business people have created small cracks in the market. Some protected those markets as they grew; others just faded away. Let's look at some specific examples.

Market Creation Examples

General Electric is an interesting and highly instructive study of survival through successful adaptation over the years. The notion that Thomas Edison started GE is, at least partly, business mythology. Thomas Edison owned and built—on the basis of his very famous inventions—-the Edison Company. He created many innovations in several areas. Of course, the most notable was his invention of the light bulb, completed and marketed in 1879. He went on to come up many hundreds of innovations for manufacturing the light bulb, which he also patented to prevent copycats from competing.

Direct current (DC) electricity was already the driving force behind his many innovations. Westinghouse was an intense competitor with Edison in those years. But many small innovative

> **A kind of spontaneous combustion exists around certain developments throughout history when several visionaries see the same crack in the market developing.**

companies were in direct competition with Edison to provide electric power and lighting to businesses and consumers. One such company was the Brush Electric Company. Charles Francis Brush had developed his own generator (he called it a "dynamo") that powered a very bright light called an arch light (due to the way electricity was arched across two metallic points) to create an intense light. These lights could light up several blocks from a single high pole. Brush installed a complete power generating and lighting system in San Francisco in 1879.[5]

You can see, therefore, that the use of electricity was envisioned by many people at the same time. A kind of spontaneous combustion exists around certain developments when several visionaries see the same niche developing in the market. Electric power, like steam power before and the computer market since, was one of those watershed moments where many recognized the potential at the same time. Edison was perhaps the most famous, and clearly an innovative genius of his time. But he was not unique.

Just as brilliant was Nicola Tesla, a young immigrant who wanted to work for the famous Thomas Edison. But Tesla and Edison were like fire and water. Tesla, a formally trained scientist, could not communicate with the famous tinkerer-entrepreneur, and was easily hired away by Westinghouse.[6] During the famous "War of the Currents" fought between Edison Electric and Westinghouse over AC and DC power formats, both spent money on demonstrations and lawsuits against each other during the late 1880s. The battle was over which electric standard would be used in the many thousands of new projects that would transform the world through the use of electric power. This was a battle larger than the battle for operating systems during the initial computer period. By the early 1890s both Edison and Westinghouse were weary and cash depleted when they competed for the new lighting contract for the electric exposition at the 1893 Columbia Exposition in Chicago.

They were so preoccupied that a small company in Redlands, California actually solved the power debate by building the first modern three phase power plant. Thompson Houston Electric had worked on the same issues for power generation to run motors and lights and was competing with Edison and Westinghouse to build the three-phase generator and five three-phase motors. Thompson Houston solved the problem first.

The early electric companies were not the only ones watching this monumental economic explosion. The financial people were also attentive. J.P. Morgan was a giant among giants in financing companies of that era. It was J.P. Morgan who financed stock ownership, and a consolidation between Thompson Houston and The Edison Company, to build a brand new company we now know as General Electric. Morgan had noticed that Charles A. Coffin, of Thompson Houston, had made over twice the profit that The Edison Company had earned (26% vs. 11% net profit) so he put Coffin in charge of the new company. The rest is history. Of course Edison, through General Electric, did win with his light bulb which quickly killed the relatively dangerous Brush Arch light. But the three-phase electric motor became America's new horse power and transformed the world. In one stroke, J.P. Morgan turned the electric power industry into a huge market. He understood all the components of electric power production required to develop the industry and also recognized that appliances were needed to <u>consume</u> electricity. Morgan built GE by gobbling up several niche markets for transmission, motors, lighting and soon small appliances.[7]

Many new niche markets were created by a host of innovative companies, all trying to jump into a niche that they hoped would grow, and that they would benefit from. Some actually did. GE, of course, became a major motor manufacturer and kept that crack for many years, although today it is no longer an impressive player in the motor and electric business. It is still a major turbine manufacturer, however, one among a few worldwide. Others remain too, in various electric niches created by this new huge industry. Many more saw opportunities to engineer products or systems in a crack that others did not see, including: long distance power transmission, consumer appliances, hydropower, irrigation, and countless other components that involve electric power today, including the computer!

Once these new cracks were filled, additional would-be entrants had a difficult time trying to gain a foothold. Many who tried were outgunned by companies that already had plants, cash, marketing power and personnel to innovate.

Creating or occupying an empty crack is always easier than waging war on a crack that has been filled.

Finding Your Crack In The Market

ANCO International

Most companies that create a new crack are small. ANCO, a privately held company founded in 1986 in San Bernardino, is an example of a basic industrial business that slowly developed a crack for specialty valves and hose couplings. Marjorie Nielson took over the machine shop following her husband's sudden death. She struggled to keep the business going, to serve customers and to sell machining services and products. Not a machinist herself, she was open to listening to and solving customer problems. She discovered the need for hose couplings that were adapted for specialized industries. Slowly, through trial and error, she found new solutions to new or emerging problems.

As the company found and developed customers, it expanded into different types of hose couplings; many were highly specialized and needed only very in small quantities. Although most standard application hose couplings are now made in China, the company learned how to make money on very small custom orders, designing different applications for moving different kinds of liquids in hoses. ANCO became expert in solving these problems, and charged fair prices (lower than ANCO could have demanded, given its specialization). In particular, ANCO engineers listened to customers about the difficult hands-on issues that needed to be solved. Trust developed and was maintained with customers over two decades. Today her son, Bill Hosier, who grew up in the business, has an uncanny ability to solve coupling problems that involve three-dimensional manufacturing issues. ANCO has developed multiple, very small crack niches around its core competence of machining, knowledge of the liquid transfer industry and a unique ability to look for solutions that big competitors simply cannot handle. These small niches provide enough additional margin on the products to maintain a healthy company despite the inefficiencies inherent in custom production. The result is that ANCO makes the only couplings for several niche applications in the world.

Esri, Environmental Systems Research Institute

In the early 1980s, Scott Morehouse, a young programmer at the Harvard Laboratory for Computer Graphics and Spatial Analysis, conferred over lunch with a landscape architect. A project he had come up with to improve GIS (Geographic Information Systems) was being defunded, just when he thought it was showing promise. The general concept was to develop shapes to represent spatial data. Measurements of a park, for instance, could be represented by boundaries, contours, and images representing trees and bushes, and so forth. The landscape architect either recognized the potential for his own business or understood the programmer's vision for what might happen when fully developed.

With a few years of programming and much more analysis, an innovation was born for representing data in a spatial format — that is, to build maps, contours, roads, and structures, on a computer screen, directly from data, instead of "drawing" it on a screen. This is a powerful concept. Scott Morehouse and Jack Dangermond, another former Harvard Lab researcher, have become famous for this in their market niche. The application today can be used for environmental planning, urban planning, sophisticated mapping, driving directions, and many more wonderful uses. The GIS industry was born and, being first with a commercial product, Esri soon owned the market. Esri had no competitors and had created a completely new way to analyze mapping (and spatial) data.

Esri's rapid growth over the years, and innovative software captured many large governmental and geographic uses over the first decades of the GIS business. This growth pattern, like General Electric's, is instructive of how small market crack players can make huge profits fast enough to capitalize large businesses that can maintain larger cracks they create in the market. We will discuss more about market types in the next chapter.

> **The Golden Fleece in business is when a company is perfectly emplaced in a niche such that it can attain leadership. Great profits can follow even lacking management genius.**

When you own patents, control a niche market, or provide high value products with low cost profiles, you can make lots of money. (Please see the discussion of Profit Impact of Market Strategy (PIMS) in Chapter 6 for more information on this.) Creating a crack in this type of market is the highest level of strategic market thinking. It is **market emplacement** and positioning. The rest of marketing is all sales and promotion. Of course, keeping your niche can be challenging; but at least when you face very little competition, a business model exists to fund your growth.

Companies that are in the "best of niche" market emplacement can prosper despite many inefficiencies. This position can be maintained as long as the value proposition is not compromised. That is, as long as your customers (most of the buyers in your niche) perceive the value of your product and they have little other alternative, your business can maintain very high prices and extraordinary profits, even if this process is inefficient. Well positioned and emplaced companies are not always well-oiled businesses. They can be extremely wasteful and very poor at "marketing" and still succeed. Many smaller businesses fit this description, at least for a time period.

Some innovators recognize an opportunity in an existing or brand new market. Thomas Edison is highly celebrated for his serial inventions of new products that were immediately embraced by customers. The Edison Company did provide company growth and wealth for him. But he made as many poor decisions as good ones; we just remember his light bulb, phonograph, motion photography and other high profile consumer inventions. His visionary persona missed the true genius of his employee, Nikola Tesla. Edison was determined to develop Direct Current, while Tesla saw its limitations and developed Alternating Current. Edison eventually lost that battle with Westinghouse (with Tesla at his side) and so drained the company that J.P. Morgan had to rescue it.

Indeed, when Morgan started GE, he refused to allow Edison any day-to-day decision making power in the new company. Charles A. Coffin, its founding president, was a skilled business man, known as "a man born to command, yet who never issued orders." It was the culture of business brought by Coffin that would guide the modern corporation with professional business management. Many company founders fall into the same trap that Edison did: they measure their success based on sales volume or profit, thinking themselves very smart, when in reality, they simply filled their market crack well. Market innovation is a task to be celebrated; but it does not necessarily mean the founder is a great business person.

Some cracks are created by people of great vision; some are mistakes that are recognized by chance; and some people are just at the right place at the right time with the right competencies.

In the business context, the Golden Fleece is when a company is perfectly emplaced in a niche such that it can attain leadership. Small businesses can create great wealth when they control a niche market whether or not they are well managed.

Longmont Dairy

Small cracks can be expanded into larger ones. In 1989, David and Susan Boyd saw an opportunity to live the rural community lifestyle they loved. They took over the recently closed Colorado dairy of David's retired father and partner. They bought a small herd, rented a farm, rented an old processing plant, and began to rebuild a niche business, home delivery of dairy products.

Home delivery of milk and cheese was supposedly a dying business, having been essentially ravaged by supermarkets since the 1960s. But by the 1990s, the market had shifted again. Many households now had the advantage of two incomes. The college educated families lived in the suburbs and commuted to work. In addition, "natural" and "organic" foods were developing and those concerned with natural, wholesome products were willing and able to pay for both quality and service.

Longmont Dairy rebuilt its business on this new base. The Boyds went out of their way to use reusable and recyclable glass bottles. They worked hard to maintain a very well fed, healthy herd, and promised customers that they would not stress their cows by using bovine growth hormones. The company was positioned to customers as the wholesome, convenient alternative to shopping at a large supermarket. Its branding was carefully constructed to communicate specific company values to those most likely to be customers. As the only home delivery company in the Longmont and Boulder area, the differentiation was easy.

As the company grew from a few thousand customers to tens of thousands of customers, its geographic area began to push into the competition's traditional cracks in Denver. The competing home delivery dairies, at this time, were many times larger than Longmont Dairy. Moreover, while the competition was aware of Longmont Dairy, its leaders doubtless thought little about it at first. Part of the reason was Longmont's strategy of keeping its head down. Of course, the milk box on the porch makes quite plain who has the milk delivery service; but during this period where the territory overlapped, Longmont Dairy tried hard to play "small and dumb." Trucks were modest and the plant looked dilapidated from the outside. The office was very basic and unassuming. While market share was growing, the Boyds did no public advertising, relying instead on internal communications via a cute newsletter to develop loyal customers. As the dairy grew, its profits and finances did too. The owners maintained a very modest lifestyle, building plenty of financial strength for the battle they assumed would eventually come.

Slowly the Longmont crack strengthened geographically as it added an adjacent community. The competition, having a very large geographic area to occupy and protect, could easily make its sales quotas by working in areas far from Longmont's market. In any case, the real differentiator was the value offered to the upscale customer: wholesome milk from the Boyd's own cows, no growth hormones, true environmental sensitivity, great quality and service, delivered in reusable glass bottles. The customer was paramount.

One crack after another was invaded—much like trench warfare. Longmont Dairy bought out a small dairy in a western Denver suburb and quickly filled the gaps. Then, carefully avoiding neighborhoods that would be tough to deliver in, the Boyd's encircled Denver itself. The larger competition still has plenty of business, because as often happens in small niche markets, more people come to understand the product when there are several suppliers. The two dairies now compete with each other.

Over 10 percent of fluid milk is bought from home delivery trucks in the Denver market today. But Longmont Dairy is now a very formidable player, fighting block by block for a share of its market. It has financial resources to hold out in tough years, develops the very best online marketing tools, which lowers its costs, while providing better customer service and professional materials for its well-trained sales force. Over two decades, Longmont Dairy has grown ten-fold, following principles outlined in this book.

The competition will probably continue on-again and off-again for years; but both companies have a real opportunity to thrive. With only two in the market place, they compete on value (different value scenarios, and marketing positioning) so consumers have a choice. But both know that they must maintain margins too, so prices are not really the differentiator. Marketing differentiators and perceived value can create brands that customers come to trust, even when buying what is considered a commodity.

New entries in a market like this are very difficult indeed. Others have tried, with nothing special about their operations other than their trucks are painted differently. Startups try to gain a foothold in a very local area, but can't get a foothold large enough to create efficiencies. And although efficiencies are not necessary in a high price context, they <u>are</u> important in a low price, high service requirement business. New entrants in an existing market must have clearly defined advantages to the customer to battle established brands. We will return to this in Chapter 7, "The Value of Marketing Value."

Over two decades, Longmont Dairy has grown ten-fold, following principles outlined in this book.

Chapter 4   Market Types

Three types of markets exist: mature markets, rapidly growing markets, and new markets. New markets can be truly "new" or can collide with mature markets, thereby disrupting the old market.

Just Three Ways to Grow

You can only grow your business revenue three ways: increase your share in a mature market (that is not declining), be in a growing market and grow with the market; or create a new market and keep a sufficient market share. Each division, product category, or even product has its own market; each needs to be evaluated at that level. Planning for growth requires knowledge about each of these markets at the appropriate level. A few lucky businesses can easily determine which type of market they are in because they have a single product or serve a single market. For the rest, figuring out optimal strategies requires some thought and investigation, and several different marketing strategies may emerge.

These several strategies will require specific marketing campaigns, with appropriate activities and communications targeted to the specific customer segment. Since every company has limited resources, understanding exactly what type of market a product falls into, and where to put those resources, assists in the long-term stability of the business. As simple as the three ways to grow business may sound, the reason few businesses do a good job of planning for growth is the complexity of planning multiple markets with different strategies.

While it's easy to get lost in the process, such confusion is not at all necessary. Planning should be reduced to a normal operational function. Once the process is determined and the goals set, the marketing planning can simply follow the road map. The marketing and sales departments can thus build campaigns with a much better chance of success and measurement. So, let's first look in detail at the three ways to grow your business.

The Stagnant Market

Good growth is inflation plus several percentage points. A stagnant market is one growing at, or just above, the inflation rate. In a stagnant market, the only way for business to expand is by stealing business from competitors, which is accomplished through a concerted effort to increase the customers' perception of your quality, price, service and image. Pressure on margins in stagnant markets can be intense. Some companies take the low price approach. The only ones that win the low price game are those that can produce for less, usually because they also have the most volume. Each product niche will have just one low price winner.

Other companies look at the total value of the product and attempt to differentiate products through perceived quality, service or image. In a mature market, companies tend to consolidate as margins get thin. The big fish always eat the smaller ones.

The Expanding Markets

Many fortunes are made because a market is expanding. The cell phone market was an example of an expanding market, when sales of a product or category of products can grow easily by simply keeping up with general trends. Many companies can grow, but only the best grow faster than the general rate of growth. If your market is expanding at 10 percent per year, and your business is only growing at 8 percent, it is not necessarily a good year. Sooner or later growth markets begin to mature and then only the strong brands, or the best managed, survive as the market stabilizes. Today the cell phone market is being taken over by the smart phone. And already the smart phone market is consolidating. Over time, only a few (operating systems) will survive, ending the expanding market and demonstrating the mature market.

Table 1 . Characteristics of the three market types.

	Growth Goals	Growth Performance	Margin	Advantages	Dis-advantages	Value Profile
Stagnant Market	Must steal business to grow	Inflation plus several percentage points	Very competitive – volume assured	Slow moving	Very competitive	Low Cost
Growth Market	Must grow faster than market	Market growth plus several points	Good margin opportunity	Easy growth	Draws new competition	Production and distribution oriented – High perceived value a plus
New Market	Must cover entry costs – all other growth a plus to business	Beat inflation – must grow fast enough to meet demand or attract new competition	Excellent opportunity for good margins	No competition	High cost for development – high risk	High creativity and deep understanding of customer needs

A New Market

Creating a new market includes inventions, innovations and newly configured services and products. It can also include new approaches to niche markets. When this is successful, a business can grow as fast as the market the invention creates. It can afford rapid growth, but attracts attention and more competition. Companies that solve customer problems with unique solutions, or new combinations of services and products, create their own products with *private* niche markets. (Private markets are those with no competitors).

While few inventors (some say less than 1 percent) ever reap the rewards of a new product, many companies are adept at re-fashioning existing markets into new niche markets where they create new business. This is a little different than just adding a brand to a product in another niche. Rather, a product is slightly modified to create a different niche. Apple recently introduced the new, lower priced, multi-colored iPhone 5c to create a new market in the Third World. John Porter, a professor at the University of Illinois, is working on computer chips built not on silicon, but degradable "cellophane," so chips can be flexible and therefore wearable. They will degrade for applications where you do not want the "computer" to survive, such as sensitive information, or internal organ monitors following an operation.

Spending money on an expensive image campaign in a high growth, "low price is winner" market can be a waste of resources. However, in a highly competitive, stable market, the skillful use of company aesthetics can mean a differentiation that more than pays for the effort and increases business revenue and gross margins.

Absolut Vodka is a case in point. Years ago, before development of the different flavors now available, to most people vodka was vodka. But judging from its incredible performance in the U.S. in the nineties, consumers must have thought Absolut was better. The only difference was the aesthetic difference — the contemporary bottle. Without this differentiation, a vodka maker had to compete with price and in-the-trenches competition in the distribution channels.

Catching Smirnoff completely by surprise, Absolut changed the vodka market by capturing a huge share of what had always belonged to Smirnoff. The consumer saw Absolut as the new, contemporary, "cool" vodka. The label actually caused the consumer to think it tasted differently. Today many others differentiate vodka with flavors, bottles and colors.

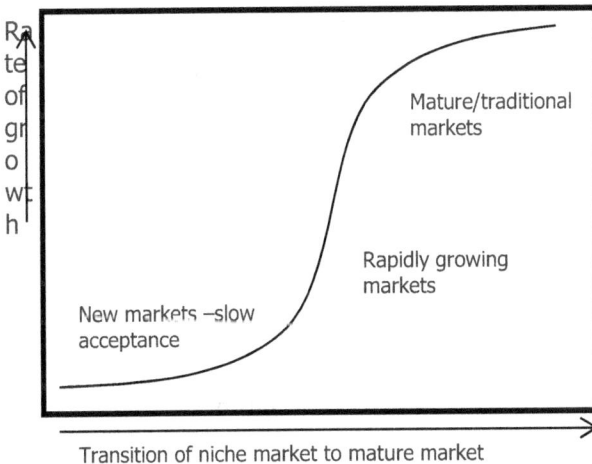

Transition of niche market to mature market

Newly created markets are normally very small cracks at first. Growing markets are usually new markets that gain substantial traction and start to grow rapidly, such as cell phones, or the personal computer industry in the 90s, or the electric power industry in the early nineteenth century. Over time they can combine into a single growth curve containing all three phases.

Another characteristic of niches is the level of competition in each. Some markets are so well emplaced that they need no marketing at all. While rare, they do exist. Imagine a desert with a single well in the middle. The owner has a monopoly, and because every camel train that comes by needs water desperately, no marketing or brand is necessary. At the other extreme, consider the challenge of selling ice to Eskimos, who all are standing on packed snow. The only cost is cutting it out and adding it to the igloo. Not only can anyone can sell it, but it is readily abundant. The old saying "he can sell ice to an Eskimo" reflects the difficulty of doing so. Sure, the right marketing or creative can create a new market (the Pet Rock), but it requires brilliance in positioning, in branding. It can be done if you are willing to innovate around the commodity and add overall value to it.

Understanding how crowded your niche is illustrates why finding your own crack in the market is so important. If you dug the well in the desert, you have already succeeded. If you are managing to sell ice to Eskimos, you are a marketing genius. But more seriously, businesses fall somewhere in between these two extremes.

Marketing promotion and advertising is a remedy for <u>poorly positioned and/or highly competitive markets.</u> Look at bottled water. Municipal water (in the U.S.) is highly regulated, while bottled water is <u>not</u>.[8] Authorities consistently vouch for tap water throughout the U.S. as the best water, including for drinking; but marketers for bottled water continue to overcome that reality despite the high cost and the environmental problem of disposing of billions of plastic bottles. This is accomplished through intensive marketing to convince people that bottled water is actually purer!

New Market Cracks

New market cracks normally have few competitors. Sometimes it's only the company that created the crack. Hundreds of thousands of these very small new cracks exist, and they are created almost daily around the world. When a market like the mobile phone starts to grow, many competitors enter the market to cash in on the bonanza. During the high growth period, many competitors can be successful; but as it slowly matures, weaker competitors withdraw as real business prowess becomes the differentiator. Normally only three or four companies survive in a highly profitable way. As these growing cracks get bigger, many smaller cracks develop off the main valley. As the market gets more crowded, products begin to morph to fill these smaller niche cracks. Mobile phones added color, more features, flip tops, larger displays; they morphed with personal digital assistants, as seen in Research in Motion, the Canadian telecommunication and wireless equipment company best known for developing the BlackBerry brand of smartphones and tablets.

Then the Apple Computer company's iPhone transformed a new crack, which will in turn split into other smaller niche cracks. The mobile phone is no longer a phone, but a small computer with a phone imbedded. As this industry slowly matures, the price pressure will begin to force some companies out of the crack entirely. As I write this chapter, Research in Motion struggles to maintain its Blackberry business in the face of the new paradigm shift in the market posed by the iPhone. Given the incredible loss of market share and revenue reduction, it remains to be seen if RIM can survive the massive chasm almost instantly created by Apple and the iPhone.

This cycle is perfectly demonstrated by the personal computer industry. When microchips were invented, a few very small companies saw an opportunity to create a very small crack, that of hobbyist computer builders. Several small companies built components for making an electronic machine that could "compute" numbers and basic instructions.

At first, this was a novelty reserved for the techie geeks (this was before computer geeks!) who understood how to build short wave radios and larger computers. The low cost chips, which replaced the much higher cost transistors and tubes of the first large computers, made this an affordable hobby.

First sold through catalogs, components could later be purchased at "computer" stores, where computer geeks could also exchange advice and assistance. Programming was required, so other small companies stepped in to create "operating systems" (such as CP/M) that provided the first layer of software to the hobbyists. Then a complete computer kit, the Apple I, was designed, followed by the Apple II, in 1977. Steve Jobs and Steve Wosniak had created the personal computer niche. Others followed, but Apple prevailed by capturing the crack it had created, at least for the time being.

Many others saw the vision. New cracks ruptured from the main personal computer crack: operating software, porting of games to the computer, accounting software, the first "Killer apps," the spreadsheet, and word processing programs. Dozens of small companies and entrepreneurs emerged as people began to understand what could be done with these small computers. I bought an Apple II for my business in 1978, became an early user of VisiCalc, and started doing our financials on it. I could compile an income statement in five hours, whirling between two external 5 inch floppy drives.

Apple overtook the market from Commodore PET, and TRS 80, by Radio Shack. Within a couple of years, noticing the growing crack in the market, IBM cobbled together the first "PC" Personal Computer, breaking its tradition of creating all components and software in-house. IBM was caught so off-guard by this new market crack that it could not respond. Small businesses were buying these PC's for business and, for the first time in two decades, IBM's key business, computing, was flanked by a few guys in this place that became Silicone Valley. IBM recognized that if it did not enter the growing market, it would be left in the lurch.

Bill Gates and Paul Allen, in the now famous IBM negotiations, leveraged their modified BASIC language by licensing it to IBM. They had licensed their operating system to several other early startups in the computer crack. In this deal, the Microsoft operating system was not exclusive to IBM, so Microsoft was able to standardize a language that would be used across several personal computers.

As could have been expected, in 1981 IBM hit the rapidly growing market with a huge national advertising campaign and, focusing on the business market, took over market share from Apple. By 1984, Apple had to create a new niche, having lost the business market, by far the largest. The Lisa, and later the Macintosh machines created a graphics friendly, mouse driven interface. Jobs declared that, if Apple could not take the educational market, his company "deserved to go broke."[9] Jobs succeeded. He reinvented the graphical interface developed by Xerox, added a mouse, and fabulous software that could run Adobe publishing software. So, although IBM forced the little company out of the business market, Apple fortunately found a new one that captivated the graphics industry and educational industry for a generation.

90

Meanwhile, in the desktop PC business, the home market slowly increased. Yet IBM was not nimble enough to persevere. Startup Compaq stunned the market with lower costs, larger hard disk drives, portability, and reliability. A few years later, Michael Dell built custom machines, ordered from catalogs and shipped to businesses, overtaking Compaq. Compaq was bought by HP; IBM sold its PC division to an Asian company; and today the world's business and home PC market is dominated by just a few huge makers. The PC business has matured although innovation still drives the next generation of products.

As the crack grew into a canyon, the flood took down many players: Radio Shack, Osborn, Commodore, Texas Instruments, Altair, and many more. Apple survives today through innovation and dedicated fans (and because of the education and graphics niche), its failures smothered by its stunning successes, the iPhone and iPad. But as the creator of the personal computer, its market share had fallen at one point to a miniscule 3 percent. It could be argued that the business it managed to develop was really a side crack in the computer market, reliant on the perception that Apple is better at handling graphics. You Apple desktop machines lovers are undoubtedly frowning at the mere thought that I say "perception" (more about perceptions in a later chapter). To you, it is true.

This desktop computer industry example illustrates one of the most important survival principles.

> *Very successful companies must occupy their respective crack in the market, to the extent that they are in the top three in perceived quality and service.*

Because buyers reward these companies, they make more money, allowing these companies to grow and force the rest to receive marginal profits or go out of business. Only one exception exists: the low cost producer.

New markets in hairline cracks in the market can become growing markets: The crack can become a wide canyon carved by a torrent of new business. They all become mature markets where the torrent calms into a lake where few thrive. Some cracks stay small, allowing small businesses to thrive. Some canyons are dominated by the innovators, but it is exceedingly rare. Microsoft and Apple are celebrated for their staying power just as much as for their innovation. They represent the innovators who were able to grow into the niche markets they created. But most small companies cannot accomplish this. They either self-destruct by going out of business or become large companies as the crack widens into a canyon.

New market cracks that grow are the big opportunities. Apple and Microsoft are two of the rare examples of companies with founders who were able to transition into big businesses. Along the way, many other innovators helped create the market, but could not make the same transition including: VisiCalc, Lotus, Commodore, Compaq, NCR, and the list is much longer.

Thousands of other companies exist in newly created market niches that do not receive the attention that the computer industry did. Most of these niches are known only by those in each industry. These are where the opportunities for the small business exist. Few end up creating enormous markets such as the personal computer business.

Chapter 5   Defining Market Cracks

Some markets may seem large until you consider the additional ways that each market is broken down. Each crack is normally defined by several factors that further limit its size, making small cracks that even small businesses can occupy and fill.

Cracks are further reduced by geography, specialization, specification, stickiness and relationship or referral.

Geography is simply the limit on a crack's ability to deliver to a locality. The contemporary Internet is usually thought to make everything global. This is true in many markets. But geography can still be very small and not subject to the Internet. My favorite example is the hot dog vendor. A large market you might think, but not if you are at a football game. Because hot dogs are poorly differentiated at football games, you will buy one from the nearest vendor. If that vendor is a commissioned hawker, he or she may actually only serve a single section and a few rows. You can go up to the corridor and stop at the crowded stand, but you'll buy the same hot dog and still have the local hawker working hard for your business. This is a micro hairline crack in the market, with absolutely no threat from the Internet or the hot dog stand across the parking lot.

Most other geographic cracks have something to do with transportation. I outlined the transformation of retail markets in U.S. history in the Introduction. Transportation still influences the shape of geographic cracks in the market. First think of the smallest market, such as the hot dog seller— any convenience category works, such as food, drink, or nails, and especially gasoline. The product may be a commodity, but the seller has a small geographic crack, where you happen to be at the time. These niches in a city are as small as a block or two, on a commercial street. Bank deposit locations play a major role for businesses that need to make deposits frequently.

A little wider geographic crack includes service niches, plumbing and home repair, carpet cleaning, etc. These services typically are local in nature as they are for most business services. A local plumber may say he serves a county; but his price is influenced by his drive and the extent of the service. The plumber will be less competitive on repairing a plugged toilet that requires an hour drive than the one down the street. So even though many say they serve large areas, most of the time smaller service providers work close to home. As the **specialization** or price of the product or service increases, the geographic niche does as well. You won't drive ten miles for a Coke, but you will drive twenty miles if you are buying office furniture or carpet for your home.

Finding Your Crack In The Market

When industrial motors need repair, the market is regional, a mix between transportation costs for heavy bulky material and the proximity of the competing repair shops specializing in rewinding electrical coils. This illustrates a larger geographic footprint, but a smaller market for motor repair than office furniture or carpet.

So the local plumber has a small crack in the local geographic market, as does the motor repair shop with a state or multi-state geographic area. You might be thinking now that you know a regional plumbing company. Sure, there is a market for larger plumbing contractors; the niche normally means they do bigger projects requiring financing, engineering, more labor—all factors that preclude the small guy from competing. But the larger commercial plumber would likely have trouble being competitive for the single stopped-up toilet. They each might think they can compete in each market; but under pressure they will withdraw from the market. (Unless, of course, they simply do not know how to measure the real cost created by such folly.)

When novice entrepreneurs have an idea for a new product, they seldom realize the constraints imposed by the existing distribution channels. For example, Snapple found distribution to be a major issue as a struggling new entrant into a niche for its new non-carbonated, natural flavored drinks. It lacked access to grocery stores, given the system of retail distributers. Snapple was forced into other distribution channels, namely the smaller specialty convenience market. Rush Limbaugh and Howard Stern were hired to promote this brand heavily, and created so much demand that Snapple was finally able to break into the monopoly of existing distributers to large stores.

The distribution chain is not open to everyone. Given the number of products available, and the time required to listen to and evaluate products, buyers listen to only so many pitches. Those already part of the "catalog line" have the advantage; once selected for distribution, the tendency is to the status quo.

I worked to gain new distributers for a double hung window balance. But it was slow going. Only when we moved distribution onto the Internet did we develop business. This "old line" product was one of the first alternatives to the classic rope and weight balance for double hung windows that had become popular in mid-1800s. Invented by an architect who built sets in Hollywood, he patented the metal spring balance in the early 1920s.

The company prospered until the double hung window lost favor in new homes in the forties and fifties. When Don and Judy McFarland bought the remaining small company, they used the Acme Duplex spring balance in their all wood window business; this is a quality product that lasts many decades. The millions of installed springs, a few of which are only now failing, are creating a unique replacement market. While we can demonstrate the replacement market, the alternatives that are already in the distribution channels create a steep hill to climb.

From the distributer's perspective, the market is too small to invest in inventory. Plus, other products are now available from competitors to lift double hung windows. So, many prefer to pass, believing they will do little business. Don has been successful in selling the balance to new window manufacturers, so the little company thrives. As the product gains additional recognition, more distributers will add the product. In the meantime the Internet provides a unique opportunity to sell one specific product to those who search for it. Now shipments go as far away as Australia.

Alternative distribution methods do exist. Turn on your television and watch all those infomercials. Many of these are for products that could not break into the traditional distribution channels of the wholesale and retail worlds. Malcolm Gladwell, in his book "What the Dog Saw," tells the story of the "Pitchman" Ron Popeil and his Ronco company.[10] No market could be more crowded than that of kitchen appliances. But who hasn't heard of the Dial-O-Matic, Chop-O-Matic, and Veg-O-Matic? These classic kitchen tools revolutionized the kitchen.

Far from gimmicks or cheap plastic choppers, these appliances were studied carefully and developed in the family kitchens over years of trial and error. Gladwell says of Popeil and his company: "They believed that it was a mistake to separate product development from marketing, as most contemporaries did, because to them they were indistinguishable: the object that sold best was the one that sold itself."

Coming from a long family line of boardwalk pitchmen dating as far back as the 1880s, Popeil "took the secrets of the pitchmen to the television screen." We have all seen the now-common infomercials on late night TV, or cable every hour of the day. Each Ronco innovation is a solution to a kitchen problem, carefully and painstakingly designed in the Popeil family kitchen. But their other innovation was turning the pitch into a science, one that carefully took each observer through each problem to be solved, and then carefully laid out the solution and the easy way to order and pay for the appliance.

Can creating a niche for a single product work? Ron Popeil saw problems with kitchen rotisseries. Nothing on the market roasted all meats perfectly every time. He spent months in his kitchen trying different ideas, tweaking the speed, improving product components, creating the perfect even golden brown skin. The result was the "Showtime Rotisserie." Here is how the great story teller Gladwell describes it:

"It was 12:40 a.m. In the studio, Ron was slicing onions with one of his father's Dial-O-Matics. [His wife, Shannon] looked at the second monitor and gave a little gasp. Forty minutes in, and Ron had already passed $700,000. A QVC manager walked in. It was 12:48 a.m., and Ron was roaring on: $837,650. "It can't be!" he cried out. "That's unbelievable!" Two QVC producers came over. One of them pointed at the first monitor, which was graphing the call volume." Jump," he called out. "Jump!" There were only a few minutes left. Ron was extolling the virtues of the oven one final time, and sure enough, the line began to take a sharp turn upward, as all over America viewers took out their wallets...."You know, we're going to hit one million dollars, just on the first hour," one of the QVC guys said.... At that moment, on the other side of the room, the door opened, and a man appeared, stooped and drawn but with a smile on his face. It was Ron Popeil, who invented a better rotisserie in his kitchen and went out and pitched it himself. There was a hush, and then the whole room stood up and cheered."[11]

Even in a highly competitive market, opportunities exist when new cracks are discovered and exploited.

Specification

Another type of crack that further breaks down markets is specification. The Acme Duplex spring balance is again an example. Market specification exists where a very specific part, tool or service is required to complete or repair a product. Manufacturers love to be the only ones with replacement parts for an appliance. That means that consumers can only buy from the authorized dealer. In turn, the authorized dealer can only sell in a specified geographic area. Generally the hassle for a "work around" is too great to worry about the price. You may not like it (and the product may not even be very good), but you decide to go forward with the repair in light of the replacement cost of the whole appliance.

The infamous examples are the "foreign" car with only original parts available for replacements; matching old cabinet hardware and internal replacement parts for water faucets. Undoubtedly you can add many more.

Each decision made considers the cost of part replacement compared with the total product replacement. The pricing model for the part is not based on the cost to manufacture it, but on the value to the consumer who is determining the complete replacement cost. As consumers, we hate this situation. Nonetheless, it is a great market crack to occupy, until consumers spread bad news about your company and damage your brand. Don't get too greedy in this market.

Stickiness

Specification is similar to **Stickiness**, where leaving a service is more pain than it is worth. Credit and banking accounts, and especially electronic accounts, are so hard to close and move that we are *stuck* with them, unless we are truly upset or not having highly important needs met. Stickiness and Specification niches allow all kinds of ineptitude with little risk of going out of business. Normal competition here does not apply: each product or service becomes a micro-niche, because change has cost.

Until recently the cable TV business was very sticky. Switching cable service was hard because of long term contracts and the lack of alternatives. The cable companies were very successful in making the case that their capital costs were so huge that each city should grant long term contracts protecting them from competition. When satellite TV became competitive, the cable services finally lost some stickiness when contracts ran out. Today the Internet is also providing competition to cable, so most of us will have several easy opportunities to switch. This was an example of government-sanctioned stickiness. Software has become very sticky. Once your data is in QuickBooks, a relational database, or Adobe InDesign, changing software can be a real pain, and costly, too. As you look around, you can see it in other markets too.

"The Relationship Niche"

Many people tell me that their markets have very large valleys, and are without cracks. The life insurance business is "just dog eat dog." Many independent insurance brokers, financial planners, CPAs, and attorneys prove the point, in my view. The small crack in the market is still defined by geography, but the **Relationship** crack further defines this niche. People make decisions in these markets based on knowledge (quality), personality and most of all *relationship*. People and companies do business with those they like and trust. I acknowledge that, starting out, the market is tough. But one at a time, very slowly at first, as these professionals get to know people, the trust and familiarity they create also creates their individual market. These micro-cracks in the market are literally created through having a relationship. While a broader market exists for financial planning, the individual market is created through the relationship.

As the relationship builds, the bonds become so tight that the customer is no longer out in the market. The business is almost completely protected by the relationship (this is defensive emplacement). People who cannot form strong relationships in such businesses do not prosper. They work for someone who has good relationships, or find another vocation. This is evidenced by the 90 percent who fail. Marketing for this group is interesting. I am told I can't be helpful unless I "go find new prospects." But prospecting efforts are extremely difficult precisely because the provider needs to fish in the relationship pond, not the general market. Sad to say, many new professionals are duped into extensive and costly direct mail programs using costly brochures when they should focus on building relationships in the community. Marketing does play a small part in supporting the development of relationships. But it is a different type of crack, one needing a different approach.

Referral and Symbiotic Cracks

The **referral** and **symbiotic** cracks in the market are similar, or subcategories, of the relationship cracks. Referrals are made to friends based on a long standing reputation or a relationship. This crack depends on the relationship of the business to the referral giver. The happy recipient can also have different cracks; but the referral comes from success in another type of niche. The symbiotic niche is when a business caters to another business and receives referrals continually like the motor re-builder I mentioned earlier. This is a nice place to be. But don't ever mess this relationship up, or you can be out of business.

Finally, a few niches are defined simply by **authenticity**. Antiques and old homes are authentic: they become increasingly rare. Ancient pubs in Britain are authentic, even though we try to re-create them in the U.S. Only the hundred year old, great tourist lodges in national parks are authentic, but thousands try to copy them. Disneyland is authentic as Disneyland; but it never really replaced Coney Island. Coney Island is an authentic amusement park. Disneyland is a copy.

Authenticity exists in certain restaurants that cannot be duplicated. We stayed in a small rough lodge outside of Kings Canyon, California built in 1948. It has not changed. While the lodge is not for everyone, its niche is authenticity; otherwise they would never be competitive. Route 66 still has several authentic motels of the 30s and 40s, and only Boston can be Boston.

Small Business Niche Markets
General Industry

Geographic

Specialization

Specification and Stickiness

Distribution Control

Referral and Symbiotic

Relationship

Authenticity

Each dimension of these niche markets creates smaller and smaller niches of just a few products or businesses. When they all intersect, millions of tiny hairline markets exist. It's like looking at cells through a microscope.

Other variants may also define small markets. The illustration shows you that many millions of small cracks in the market exist when properly viewed; and thousands of new hairline cracks appear every year.

The important take away from this chapter is a new way of looking at your market. Don't see it as merely carpet laying, or motor repair, or group insurance. It's more like a commercial carpet store located in a town or two. It's a specialization in high powered AC generators in the Northwest. It's group insurance sales for companies between 25 and 100 employees, most of whom you have a relationship with. It's a custom solution for a single pump hose coupling.

Niche Industry
Geographic
Distribution Control
Relationship
Authenticity

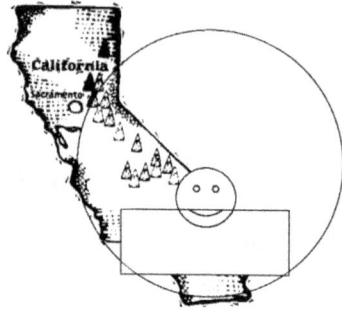

In the illustration above, the niche industry is represented by the circle. California is the geographic niche. The rectangle represents the distribution channel control, and the smiley face, of course, represents the relationship. Authenticity is represented by the smile itself. So the niche is the very small area represented by the very small smile bounded by the rectangle. Add specification and stickiness (not shown) and you see how small niches really are. Given the huge variables in each market and geographic area, millions of niches exist and are being re-named or invented every day.

I am continually amazed at the ways businesses create revenue in cracks that seemingly only they and their customers have ever heard of. One of my clients made computer chips for old battle tanks for the military. The price for one? Sixty thousand dollars. The price for two: sixty thousand and ten dollars. The geographic market was the world, but they had only two or three competitors.

104

Finding your crack in the market includes rethinking the real size of the market. It requires careful examination of your true core competencies. Then the crack becomes malleable—something you can change and restructure. When you make good decisions about your crack in the market, you can (re)fashion your business model for much higher odds of success. Conversely, when you don't understand your market, or think it is broader than it is, your resources are spread thinner across the market, removing the intensity of your advertising coverage and message. Servicing geographic areas where you do little business also increases your costs.

The overlay of a niche industry, geography and distribution control, with specification, stickiness, and relationship niches, creates micro-cracks in the market that allow even the smallest business to control their small niche. Each of these market niche characteristics influences how you can fill your own smaller crack in the market. Several of them are in play in every market. Used together, a company can fashion a smaller niche *intentionally* in order to compete better. The reasons why owning your cracks can produce huge advantages for your business are discussed in the next chapter.

Chapter 6   Customers Reward Companies That Are Better in Their Crack in The Market

Management fads and fashions come and go. Most of these new management strategies, initiatives and processes are accompanied by claims of all manner of business improvement and growth. While some include the desires of customers, many focus on business processes and techniques that are far removed from the final product or service delivered to the customer.

This chapter covers research that deals directly with customer perceptions of companies and products. It examines the effect of market and marketing strategy on the customers themselves, by looking at the actual performance of a company.

What is the Profit Impact from a Marketing Strategy?

One of the reasons that marketing is so misunderstood and its performance is doubted is that seat-of-the-pants decisions lead to poorly determined ideas that get taken over by the "creatives." Yet creative people rarely spend the years necessary to understand the optimal use of strategic marketing positioning. Most seasoned business people are well aware of the relatively simple principles of applying costs against revenues to create profit. But few understand the known principles of marketing strategy that directly point to the position in the market that creates profitable companies. This requires blending a little art and science to attain the best mix of tactics and creative work. This chapter will give you some simple but powerful knowledge of why some businesses are more successful than others.

Profit Impact of Market Strategy (PIMS) refers to a unique database that was initiated at the Harvard Business School in 1972. General Electric and each of the dozen or so other founding companies contributed marketing data and had access to all the data. Today PIMS is a vast database with hundreds of data variables from hundreds of companies and thousands of SBU's (Strategic Business Units, or divisions). It is managed by The Strategic Planning Institute.[12]

PIMS analysis considers operating expense ratios, relative quality, capital intensity, marketing expenses and other factors to understand the impact of market share and market position on profit and return on investment. PIMS includes marketing information, not just financial information. Analyzed together, this data set reveals the elements of marketing success; they bring to the fore outcomes and trends, showing high probabilities of the likely effects. These are not pure facts so should not be applied blindly. Still, they should be part of every marketing strategy discussion.

Customers rated firms as "better" or "worse" for service. When customer ratings were compared with actual performance of those firms, valuable principles emerged.

- "Better" were able to charge more for same goods
- "Better" grew twice as fast
- "Better" picked up 6 percent market share/year
- "Better" had 12 percent higher return on sales
- Quality is a consistent indicator of competitive position.

The profit impact of market attractiveness:

- **Real market growth** helps profitability a little.
- **Investment intensity** hurts profitability a lot. Investment intensity is the amount of capital investment required to enter and maintain the market. A steel plant is highly intensive while a software company is much less so.

The profit impact of competitive strength:

- Market leadership pays. Be number one or number two in your served market.
- Competing on quality is better than competing on price.

The top quintile (20%) of companies with relative quality produced Return on Investment of 32% compared with 15%. Profit was twice as much for the top quintile as for the lowest quintile.

Relative Quality (percentile)

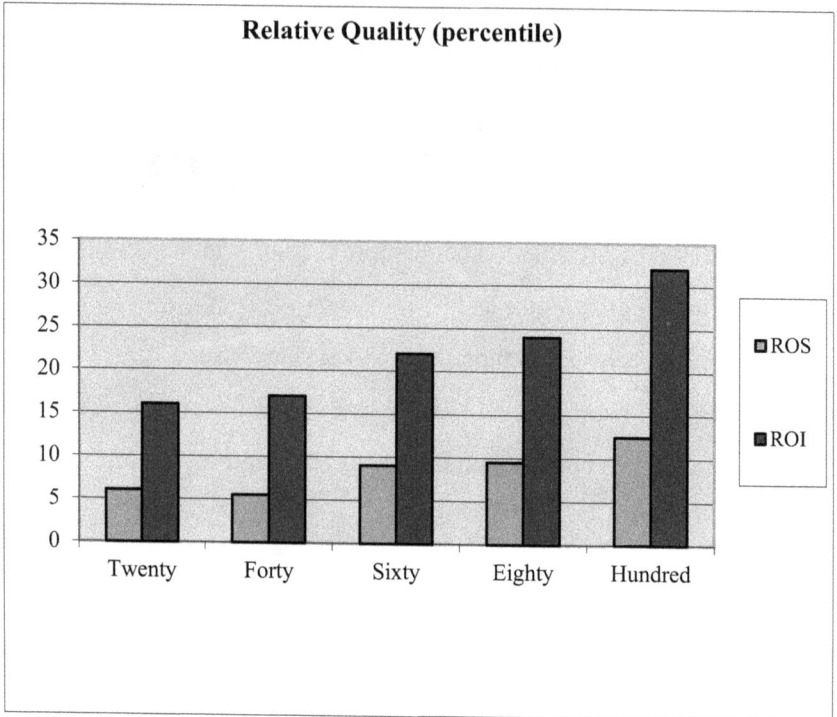

However together, relative market share and relative quality produce a huge difference in profit performance. PIMS data show that quality affects relative price; but, separate from quality, market share has little effect on price.

The top third of companies in market share AND quality had a 38 percent Return on Investment (ROI) compared with 20 percent in the middle and just 7 percent at the lower end.

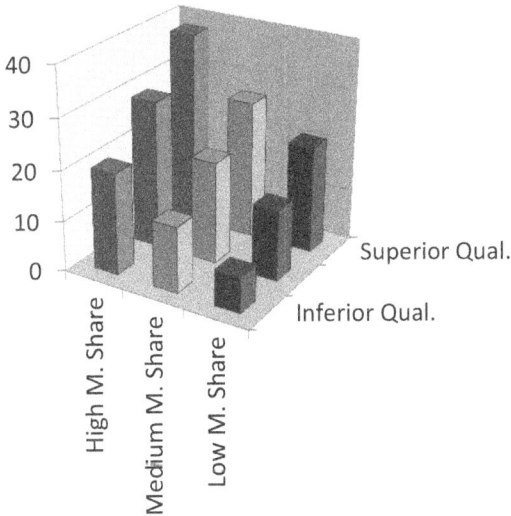

This shows that companies with higher customer perception of quality and also have higher market share, have returns 300% better than lesser companies.

However, small businesses with small market shares can and do excel if they are favorably positioned on other key strategic dimensions. The average ROI of small share businesses, whose products or services ranked in the top third in terms of relative quality, was 18 percent. If this group benefitted from low investment intensity, high labor productivity [corporate culture] and rapid market growth, its expected rate of return could easily be 25 percent or better.

Quality and Profitability

Whether the profit measure is return on sales or return on investment, businesses with a superior product/service offering clearly out-perform those with inferior quality. Several key benefits accrue to businesses that offer superior quality, at least as perceived by customers:

- Stronger customer loyalty

- More repeat purchases

- Less vulnerability to price wars

- Ability to command higher relative price without affecting share of market

- The ability to sustain price

- Lower marketing costs

Vertical integration can enhance the profitability of dominant businesses.

Quality as a term and measurement includes both the physical quality and the delivery (or service) of the product when applicable. The PIMS data shows that customers are willing to pay for high quality over mediocre quality, and good service performance over poor service. Customers vote with their money as well as their attitudes.

The PIMS data supports the notion that investments in systems and people that create perceived quality and deliver great service <u>do in fact</u>

112

have a high pay back. But some companies see the PIMS principles, as well as other customer focused benchmarks, as the driving force for survival in tough markets, not merely an investment that creates a financial return. General Electric had the benefit of this information for many years before other companies did. GE has a well-known policy instituted by former CEO Jack Welch: any division that dips to third in its market will be sold. GE maintains its high return by eliminating businesses that fail to become high performers, that is, *if they have not gained the number one or two spot in the market.*

Smaller companies have a less clear idea of where they actually fit into a market place. However, the principles derived from these landmark (and still little known) principles and benchmarks can still provide strong guidance for small companies seeking to stay competitive, and determine how to spend scarce funds and capital. Many management techniques for total quality or continuous improvement have merit. Nonetheless, an emphasis on taking care of the customer, by understanding and reacting to customers' assessments of quality and service, seems clearly the most direct path to profits.

Applications to Small Business

Most of the businesses comprising the PIMS database are large. My observations suggest that small businesses use similar metrics. Many large businesses started as small

> **The genius was the innovation and positioning, not administration, not management and not promotional prowess.**

businesses focused on their specific crack in the market. If they attained a predominantly positive perception of leadership, quality and service, they gained the PIMS advantages. They increased business market faster, made more money and had superior return on investment than the other ones in their market. Creating the crack, and differentiation from other cracks, created a huge PIMS advantage.

In fact the PIMS advantages allowed enough profit to compensate for mistakes in management and manufacturing; they had the money to fix these issues because customers rewarded their leadership. Early products have few competitors, so quality is a relative issue. You don't win by having the best continuous improvement program or the highest degree of "actual" quality. Instead, you win by being the one who is "better" than the alternative, who has fewer competitors in your crack in the market.

The PIMS principles help you see:

- How to approach your crack in the market through proper market positioning and emplacement
- How to use positive customer perceptions to differentiate you from your competitors
- How to better define or create new cracks that you alone, as the innovator, will occupy.

Managing Your Crack

The PIMS Principles provide strong benchmarks to work toward. They also provide the framework for successful positioning within your crack, and development of new hairline cracks.

The perceptions of better quality and better service are key. If yours is the only game in town, and customers want what you have, they will beat

> **Be among the top two or three companies in your market niche**

a path to your door, even as they curse your service or product. On the other hand, if you are not perceived as "better," you will prepare the way for your competitors to enter your crack. So to the extent that is necessary, programs that improve quality and service are important.

One of the key PIMS Principles is "Be among the top two or three companies in your market niche." This is the pathway to reaping profits. The PIMS study shows that the top two or three companies or products in a market crack, and in the top third of the quality/service group, reap the profit and ROI benefits. I have also analyzed which small companies that seek to become among the three top companies, do actually reap the benefits once they get there. PIMS states that companies can advance to number three from a lower position. I have assisted several clients to accomplish this. How? By offering different and better service, addressing specialized needs, and developing the additional skills to solve smaller niche issues.[13] The PIMS authors state: "Indeed, if the differences between a segment and the rest of a market are very great, it probably should be regarded as a separate market." In fact, I have seen that a new market can be defined specifically to become a leader in a slightly re-defined niche. As you know by now, I call this *market emplacement*, or "Finding your own crack in the market."

Jack Welch was known for his "rule" to sell any division that fell to number three or below in its market. Since GE has had access to PIMS from the beginning, I suspect that Mr. Welch had the data to supporting this concept. No doubt he could see the evidence in his own company as the divisions that were lower than number three matched the PIMS pattern for problematic performance. Further, when GE did sell off other underperforming businesses, the company maintained all the businesses that were in the top two spots in the market. So the company continued to thrive. From an investment point of view, GE took underperforming assets and re-invested in superior performing assets, making the company even more successful. Small businesses can do this much less frequently because they generally have only one line of business and assets cannot be easily sold and reinvested. Nonetheless, the point remains the same.

Al Ries and Jack Trout likewise endorse the concept of being in the top three leaders in a market. Ries and Trout highlight the relationship between market share and position on the ladder. More specifically, the top brand is often 40 percent of the market, the second has 20 percent, and the third just 10 percent. While each niche market is different, you can see that a small portion of many markets is very small indeed. If 20 brands get to share only 30 percent, you can see why Welsh and many other informed corporate leaders intend to be the leader in the market.

GE has had a history of innovation, creating its own market niches decade after decade. In the early days after the formation of GE by J.P. Morgan, GE dominated the light bulb business. It became a huge motor/generator manufacturer by using the prototype built by Thompson Houston for the first AC generator for Mill Creek No. 1. GE soon bought Hotpoint Iron Company, which became a full blown appliance company. In each electrical market niche GE had the opportunity to dominate, or sell out. Its enduring legacy should be that its management understand what niche to fill and continue to evolve those niches. Sure, GE is known for great managers and innovation. On the other hand, without understanding each market niche well, even the greatest managers fight an uphill battle; meanwhile, those business heads who own a leadership position in their niche can skate, and still do well.

The Moat Strategy

While the PIMS data provides us with definitive evidence for market strategies, it is not the only evidence. One of the world's most successful business investors, Warren Buffet, has developed a similar approach to finding companies that will provide sustained profit results. His Moat Strategy emphasizes "economic castles protected by unbreakable moats."[14] Moats are barriers to entry that competitors find difficult to compete with, or a crack in the market that is difficult to enter. For this reason, over his many years of buying companies, Buffet has also bought smaller companies, even though his company Berkshire Hathaway also has the wealth to buy large ones as well, such as Burlington Northern Santa Fe Rail Road.

The five barriers or "moats" are:

The Network Effect – a business that increases value as it increasingly connects with others, such as Facebook. I believe it also includes those connections where companies have symbiotic relationships.

Difficult to Leave – where customers lack the incentive to stop a service, such as telephone or cable service. (We call this stickiness.)

Virtual Control of a Market – a monopoly or narrow market where buyers have little choice. (We call this specialization.)

Proprietary Patents, Licensees or Brands – Coca Cola's value is more formula and brand than plants or distributors. Other intellectual property also counts.

Low Cost Producer – Companies that have developed a break-through cost production advantage, or a sales volume. This economic advantage allows them to become the low price competitor.

These five "Moat Strategy" categories overlap with the PIMS Principles and other points I have been making here. They also represent advantages caused by differences from the competitors, or market differentiators. I learned about Buffet's Moat investing strategy very late in writing this book. I am amazed at how close the Moat is to PIMS and to the principles I have discovered in my own practice. PIMS and Buffet both underscore the importance of scrupulous care in selecting and protecting your market niche crack.

Small companies can learn from these principles and success stories: shaping their niche is the key positioning and marketing function. If your business is number four in your market, the PIMS Principles indicate that you are at a significant disadvantage compared with the top three. If you remain in this position, you are likely to achieve only marginal success, grow slowly, and use your capital inefficiently. If you are in a stagnant or slowly growing crack, long-term success is doubtful. If you are in a rapidly growing crack, you might grow, but you will be losing ground compared with your competitors, because they have more margin to invest in higher quality and marketing.

But you can remedy this situation. This is where traditional marketing becomes effective. By emplacing and positioning your company in the top quality and service group, you can reverse your fate, and grow to number three. Of course, you have to change customer perception, which can be a formidable task. You may need to increase your actual quality in order to improve the perception, but you absolutely must communicate and convince your customers of this change. We will return to the specifics of this later.

Another strategy available to you is to redefine your crack in the market by differentiating your products and services from the main crack, creating a new hairline crack off the main crack. Apple has done this several times. Today Apple is creating an entirely new crack with the iPad. As we stated earlier in desk top computing, Apple's market share dropped to 3 percent. But when the market was re-defined as a design workstation, it captured the large majority of design firms in the U.S. Meanwhile, the iPad is the successful launch of an old idea worked on by Microsoft, IBM and others, but with an elegant design and innovative technology that re-defined the old niche. Apple emplaced themselves between their customers and the notion that a "pad" was just a small computer by extending the technology to communication, photography and other innovations.

Small companies can do this as well. Retailers continually respond to small market swings in fashion that the big chains and department stores miss. Years ago, a client of mine carved a new niche out of the toothbrush industry. A supplier to dental professionals, she put animals, and other types of figures kids loved, on tooth brush handles. She dealt only with dental professionals so she could grow to meet the demand, and kept an ever changing selection available to keep competition off balance. Her niche was nationally successful, at least until she began to sell to Wal-Mart. The refinement of her niche from "toothbrushes to dental professionals" to "unique and fun toothbrushes for kids to dental professionals" launched her into a smaller niche; but she then grew to dominate the niche. As a market leader, she profited, creating resources to be even more creative. Her growth allowed better sourcing: once she began to import merchandise from China, she dealt a double blow to competition on price. Line extensions can be dangerous if done incorrectly. But when they exploit your current core competencies and create new cracks, these can be an engine for growth, especially if the crack can be grown.

I begged my client not to ruin her business by selling to Wal-Mart. This broke all the rules of emplacement and marketing positioning. First, she displayed her ideas for all to see. Now her competitors knew the market was big enough to copy—because Walmart had said so. Second, she destroyed the trust of her loyal customers, who used her product to create just a little difference in their respective dental practices. Naturally the increased volume required that she spend more time managing the account and the rest of her business suffered even more. Selling to Wal-Mart almost killed her business. You probably can guess that she didn't keep the account: the low cost seller took it from her.

New hairline cracks can be nearly imperceptible. The small company Krispy Kreme Doughnuts became a Wall Street darling by simply serving very fresh hot donuts. Most people were used to the traditional donut shops, where donuts were made at 4:00 a.m. By the time most buyers ate a donut, it had cooled: They got a good donut, but not the same as if right out of the fryer. True, Krispy Kreme innovated a great concept— machinery made donuts while customers watched. Donut nuts would drive for miles to get Krispy Kreme's. They would bring two or three dozen to the office for immediate consumption. Growth was brisk, and the nearly imperceptible donut crack was altered. The hairline crack grew. Funding followed customers' near hysteria.

Unfortunately, the managers of Krispy Kreme let their reputation get a little ahead of the crack. As they pushed to grow, they entered the packaged donut business and sold to grocery stores and convenience stores. They misunderstood both the crack and the differentiation. Their *only* unique innovation was freshness. When they entered the mature market of packaged donuts, which were consumed far away and a day or two past their prime, Krispy Kreme tasted just like other good packaged donuts (but not as good as local donut stores). Customers in the outlying areas said, "What's the big deal?" Krispy Kreme is now failing in the mature market of packaged donuts. The once great brand was tarnished; the company was over-extended. What was probably regarded internally as a natural market extension was really a jump from a created market to a mature traditional one. My local grocery store no longer carries Krispy Kreme Doughnuts. No doubt the experience of the shop could not be replicated in a box 24 hours later.

Despite its later problems Krispy Kreme Doughnuts illustrates how a subtle change can create a new crack. The early success clearly put Krispy Kreme in the number one spot for fresh donuts. The recipients of the PIMS principles, Krispy Kreme prospered. It was poor brand management and executive zeal that dampened the growth.

Another way to compete with your bigger competitors is to win the value perception war. Understanding value is critical to making real changes in customer perceptions. The next chapter will discuss the components of value.

Chapter 7   The Value of Marketing Value

Creating Value in a Market Niche

The word "value" is one of those ridiculously overused words. Through advertising overuse, the word *"value"* has lost most of its value! Terms such as "*the best value*" and *"valuable gift,"* or *"valuable coupon"* become trite once they appear on every product label. Marketers constantly throw around "value proposition" and "customer value proposition," but can only define these phrases in a general way. Some experts use these terms to mean what the company tells customers they will get when buying the product — wishful thinking.

Despite how overusing the term *"value"* has undermined its selling impact, value is the measuring stick by which most buying decisions are made. Customers make "value" judgments every time they purchase something. Sometimes the decision means little to them, such as grabbing a pack of gum while paying for gas. Most consumers merely follow their previous habits; the cost differential is nearly meaningless.

Other decisions involve research and emotions, such as when buying a car or big screen TV.

To develop a good strategy against competition and to guide innovation, companies must understand customers' reasons for picking their product or company. Understanding *"value"* is also extremely useful in the process of carefully crafting product positioning and in comparing competing products. It becomes a major strategic tool in your crack in the market when battling competitors for the top spot.

Years ago, I developed a model to more easily assess the components of value as a tool to help clients understand how value is created and measured. This method has been used successfully to move management away from superficially boosting hype (*selling value that is nonexistent*). Great strategic thinkers, like Michael E. Porter of Harvard, have very detailed (and academic) approaches to this issue, which most small business people will not spend the time to understand.[15] While many good (and statistically superior) models exist for evaluating consumer attitudes about value, the Burgess Value Diamond© is an easily understood approach for probing the issue.

Value is the measuring stick by which most buying decisions are made.

Value has four components: **quality, price, service and image.** These four components are easily evaluated when comparing similar and competitive products, services, and companies. Without this breakdown, determining *overall value* can be very abstract and not particularly useful. I try to simplify the concept here. My approach may be demonstrated through the following example.

Compare the purchase of a Ralph Lauren "Polo" shirt from a high-end store selling designer clothing to buying an ordinary "knit-shirt" from Wal-Mart. Then, assign an approximate rating to each of the four components (quality, price, service, and image). The two similar products will probably be rated very differently.

	Ralph Lauren *(Polo brand)*	*Wal-Mart* *(generic brand)*
Price	*High*	*Low*
Image	*Highest*	*Mediocre to Low*
Quality	*Top*	*Good*
Service	*Attentive*	*Mediocre to none.*

If we chart them they might look like the chart below:

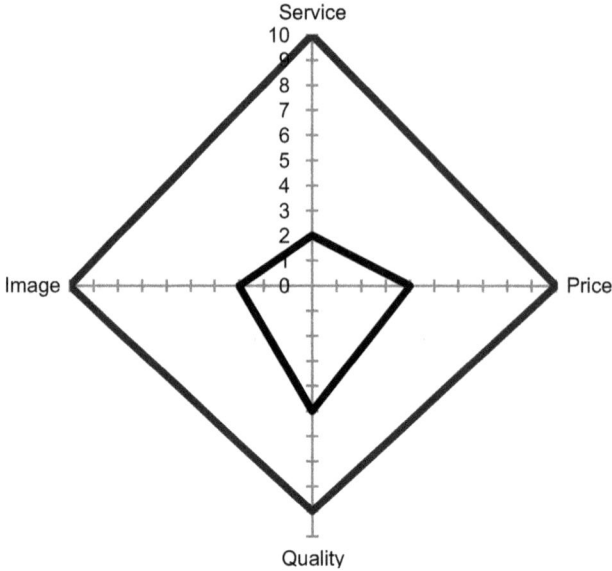

When the points are connected, a "diamond" is formed for each store's product. The larger diamond footprint represents Polo, while the smaller one represents Wal-Mart. This provides a good visual *value comparison* of the two products, revealing a considerable difference between them.

Each store has a particular market. Both stores exist in their own cracks in the market. They can exist side by side. Because of the image component, determining which is more "valuable" is difficult. One market's *perception* is that **image** is valuable. Another market's *perception* (the collective customer perception of a niche market) is that **low-price** is what matters. Just as *beauty is in the eye of the beholder,* so *value is influenced by perception.* Two markets for similar products can co-exist; both may have enough perceived value to be successful (perhaps even sharing some customers). But when you consider the discussion of market niche, you can see that few $95 Polo Shirts would sell in the very wide Wal-Mart crack. Even fewer Wal-Mart shirts would sell in a Polo Shop. (The novelty of buying a Wal-Mart shirt in a Polo Shop might sell lots of shirts, but at a great cost to Polo's image.) In fact, when you use this tool correctly, you will compare only competitors in your crack.

So when competitors are competing for the same market, value can be fashioned intentionally. I recently used this exercise to compare a client's competition.

Their chart looked like this:

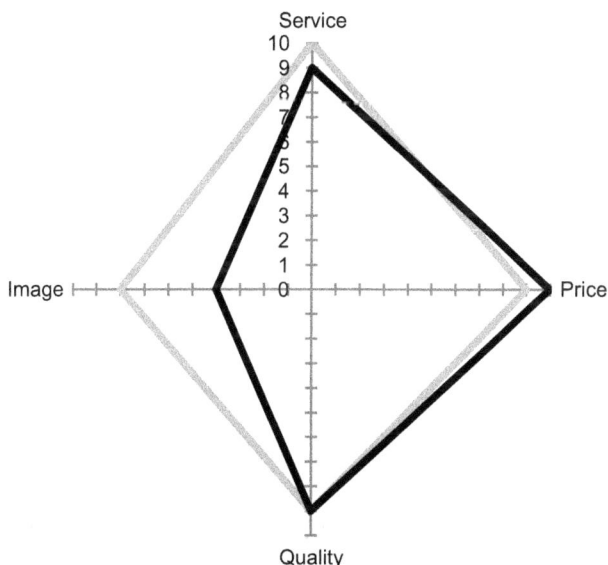

With service, quality and price so similar, the major differentiation between the two companies' value was in the element of image.

Suddenly, everyone understood the importance of maintaining consistency in all activities where the image of the company was involved.

The exact marketing positioning was deliberately raised to an increased level of importance. In this case, it became clear that projecting the wrong image might very well cause stagnation—which is a trend that is difficult to track, and expensive to discover after the damage is done.

Based on the outcome and level of examination, the Burgess Value Diamond© is useful in clarifying a variety of significant areas, including company image, product line, and service. This enables the precise crafting of an item's value while prioritizing the area that most needs the improvement or change. This method can be used to discover ways to build value into a product lacking a competitive edge (for example, a high-priced product) without the huge cost of consultancy fees or complex mathematical models.

The customer will always make buying decisions based on value. Ask yourself, "How is each of the value components perceived by my customers?" "Is a strategic plan in place for each of the components or just one or two?"

Knowing where the value lies is what is valuable in marketing!

My model is a straightforward approach to a rather difficult and complex discussion. Without understanding what components comprise value, the discussion can be convoluted. A very similar approach is used by the second largest privately owned company in the U.S., Koch Industries, Inc.

In 2007, Charles G. Koch wrote *The Science of Success — How Market-Based Management Built the World's Largest Private Company*. MBM or Market-Based Management™ is the trademarked term for the practices Koch laid out in his book. MBM has become a specific discipline. Charles Koch claims that, in just about 45 years, the MBM discipline took the company from a small business into a $100 billion behemoth.

Unlike most small business formation, the Koch brothers had a going concern to launch their business. Nevertheless, in the early 1960s due to various partner break ups, and patent law suits, the company the Koch brothers' father left them was merely a $2 million company in the oil supply business, barely making money. While the Koch brothers had a jump start that most of us don't, the growth from what was still a small business in the 60s to today is quite impressive. Today, the corporation includes companies in oil-related businesses, minerals, fertilizers, forest products, agriculture, metals, petrochemicals, and financial services.

Charles Koch says the MBM™ model is the methodology that allowed such success. Not a simple process, it includes principles from economics, social sciences, business, engineering, psychology, and management.[16] The basis of the MBM™ is creating value for customers. Not surprisingly, it includes the careful evaluation of cost, price, and quality. Koch acknowledges the importance of image and branding separately. (The Kochs own carpet manufacturing operations, which are very image conscious.)

A key concept is the understanding of value delivered to the customer in terms of delivering a product or service at the same or better quality. Koch focuses on driving down internal costs so the price to customers can fall; that is, more value is created by delivering the same quality for less money. Customer relationships and service are emphasized. In acknowledging differentiation, Koch cites Porter regarding ways to mitigate head-to-head price competition. "Generally a business person should attempt to be a price seeker rather than a price taker. This is best done by discovering new ways of creating value that is difficult to imitate."[17]

Koch states: "An effective business vision begins and ends with value creation, which is the only reason any business should exist. In a true market economy, for a business to survive and prosper long term, it must develop and use its capabilities (competencies) to create real, sustainable, superior value for its customers and for society."[18]

> **Koch states: "An effective business vision begins and ends with value creation, which is the only reason any business should exist."**

Technically this does not apply to very small businesses that simply fall into a crack that changes little or is based on location superiority or referral business. Nonetheless, all businesses should follow this mantra. It is possible, but highly unlikely, that over a long time the market will remain the same. Certainly larger markets and businesses must work on this basis, as the creative destruction of markets over time (outlined earlier in this book) always adjusts, moves, and becomes obsolete. I will point out, however, that few small businesses start out with the intent to create a multi-generational business that will survive in a crack in the market for years. Nonetheless, no business would be wrong to live by Koch's statement and achieving it would dramatically increase success over time.

Koch highlights correlations between the value of the company to the owners and the value created for customers. By creating value for customers first, you win the contract or sell the product. This in turn provides profit margin, which increases the monetary value of the company to the owners. "Customers must more highly value your products and services than the available alternatives," Koch asserts.

Creating Value

In *"The Science of Success,"* Koch defines a vision statement as the "organization's view of how it plans to create superior value for society." This includes an "assessment of its capabilities (or competencies), and the opportunities for which these capabilities can create the most value."[19]

A vision statement becomes the guiding principal for all company activity. If the perceived value of your product is superior for your crack in the market, and you effectively communicate this to your target market, you will usually win the business.

Action plans to increase value must be specific enough to guide employees to order their activities accordingly, based on management priorities.

Evaluating Each Component of Value

You will start your assessment by reviewing the Quality, Service, Price and Image of your company, then move to major revenue catagories. Ideally, each product should be evaluated, but re-sale and inventory businesses will find this too time consuming. So use the top 20 percent of your business in volume as the starting point.

Resale businesses should vet products through the inventory control process based on comparing margin, turn-over, and service costs at the SKU level. Unless one product is dependent on selling another, those products should be regularly evaluated for inventory levels.

Quality is the value component that is most often considered superior to the others. But as stated earlier, your customers buy the *perceived quality*, not the engineering specifications and tolerances that many like to call quality. Quality always depends on the overall assessment of value. Most will concede that the Polo shirt is very high quality. But that doesn't mean that every customer will value the level of quality enough to purchase the Polo shirt. This is because the customer may deem the cost too high for the quality, lowering that customer's perception of value.

A motor that has smaller tolerances for its bearings does not translate into value unless those smaller tolerances can be communicated as having a longer life or less expensive repair cost. The price will not be higher than the perceived benefit to the customer. Some engineers will argue that higher tolerances cost more to produce and therefore must push up the price. Not in a free market. Only the perceived benefit increases the amount a buyer will pay compared with the alternatives in the market.

The four components of value are in fact interdependent. All will be variable across different customers' needs and perceptions. The PIMS principles indicate that quality must be better to partake of higher margins. So failing at a comparative (higher) quality can easily pull a company into mediocrity. But remember, it is the customer who made this determination on quality. The image, and careful communication of quality through image, is what customers reference first. Then service, and later product failure, can either support or erode the perception of quality, which drives down the price.

The goal for most businesses, then, is to assure perceived quality in the top 20 percent of products, to care for your customers in a way that they regard as helpful and pleasing, while maintaining competitive or lower prices. The image drives the communications that assure that the benefits of your real level of service and quality are understood. Together these elements create the perceived value to your customers.

[For those of you who would like more information on the Value Diamond concept and how to better apply it to your company, please go online to download a whitepaper with worksheets:
www.FindingYourCrack.com/Value.htm]

Chapter 8   What does a successful small business person look like?

One of the first, but perhaps most elusive, questions about highly successful small businesses concerns the characteristics of the successful business owners. Can understanding them, and what they do, shed any light on how to achieve success? Can we learn their management and marketing secrets so that we can replicate them in our businesses?

The answer is a qualified yes, and well, not necessarily. In most cases I have studied, people who own great businesses have a strong influence in their own market niche. But this observation alone does little to help us understand who outstanding business owners are, and what they do, in a way that would point to actionable knowledge.

I like the work of Thomas J. Stanley to understand who millionaires are. His benchmark book with William D. Danko, *"The Millionaire Next Door,"*[20] helps identify characteristics of millionaires. Years ago, my first impression of this book was that "these people are my clients." Most of my clients are millionaires, and they all fit the typical millionaire profile, to the extent there is such a thing. Very successful businesses are owned by people of all races, ages, and social backgrounds, and many management styles. Increasingly, more women are part of the elite group as well. But when we sort through the research, and add another of Stanley's books, "*The Millionaire Mind*," some general characteristics do emerge.

First, of course, not all millionaires are part of our focus, those who own small business. Millionaires can develop wealth as corporate executives, well paid athletes and entertainers; less than two percent came into this category by inheriting their money. Notably, a staggering two-thirds of millionaires are self-employed.[21] Eighty percent are first generation wealthy.

Research indicates that those who are born into and raised in wealthy families do not create personal wealth at the same rate as people who need to strive. Those who are "bailed out" by parents seem to develop personalities that are not as conducive to business success. Of course, some do take over family businesses and maintain the business. But few seem to have the same "chemistry" for small business success as their parents. Interestingly, this generation does go on to college and generally does well in professional and managerial careers, outside of ownership.

Several other pertinent findings to our business discussion emerge from Stanley's work with millionaires. We can safely assume (and my research confirms) that the most successful businesses, ones that have been operating long enough to create wealth (usually over 10 years), have indeed rewarded the owner with over a million dollars of personal wealth. Most of the millionaires in the country are associated with business or professional careers.

Generally millionaires are:[22] men in their mid-fifties, who have been married for over 28 years and have a family. To be specific, 92 percent are married; and the wife, with her great budgeting skills, is a vital support to her husband.

Women seem to be gaining ground as business people; however, they still create less than a third of new businesses.[23] I have women clients who are millionaires. Women are often less visible as owners, however, because they are the wives and thus de-facto but nonetheless active partners of men who started businesses.

The recent study by the Kaufman Foundation of Entrepreneurship is important: since the late 1990s, the percentage of immigrants founding new businesses has soared. In the last few years, immigrants have founded double the number of companies as native-born Americans—a number that was about even in 1997.[24] Whether they succeed in the same proportion is not clear, but I wouldn't be surprised if they did. Immigrants appreciate the free market more than natives and very likely did not grow up as privileged as natives; as such they fit Stanley's profile of success.

Self-made millionaires tend to be frugal relative to their income and spending potential. As a result, they have very high savings and investment rates. (This prudence is where business growth investment comes from and is where jobs are created. Taxing these particular people does reduce their investment in new employees.) They own homes that are way below their means, and live in them for decades. They prefer to drive Fords over BMW's. Not your typical impression of "rich."

Stanley describes millionaires in great detail, so recounting all the juicy trivia is unnecessary. But of particular relevance here is his examination of the patterns that may drive them to becoming successful in business.

Were they all well-educated MBA's? No. In fact, while the vast majority are college graduates, as a group, they do not stack up well according to the traditional academic measures of grade point and SAT scores. The average millionaire, according to Stanley, had a GPA of just 2.9 on a 4 point scale! For business owners, it drops to just 2.76, very much in the average C+ range.[25]

Many of these business people will tell you that they thought the social aspects of college contributed more to their success than the academic ones. According to Stanley, 93 percent said that their educations were "influential in determining that hard work was more important than genetic high intellect in achieving." In other words, nearly all millionaires discount any correlation of academic success with financial success. They believe that hard work and understanding people was a key outcome of schooling.

> Getting a 2.1 on cleaning the break room is less important than getting a 4.0 on customer service.

Millionaire business owners are clearly not un-intelligent: their average SAT score was 1235. But they also felt strongly that the education they were receiving was much broader than what is typically measured with academic scores.

Other research clearly dispels the notion that success follows academic achievement.[26] This may be why J. Paul Getty, who built Getty Oil and became the benefactor of his now more famous museums, claimed that the "best thing you can do to make money, is start working immediately after high school. Don't waste time in college." He felt that getting work experience early and hard work were the paths to success. Few educated millionaires today would agree with Getty. They strongly value their educations and are willing to pay for their children's and grandchildren's educations. A college education is clearly a ticket to becoming a successful business owner.

But is there more?

These folks believe in efficiency. Stanley and Danko tell the story of a professor who gave an F^3 (read as F – cubed) for a paper that was so bad it did not even deserve a straight F! Out of 10,000 students, however, this student was the only one to argue that the professor forgot to include points for courage and perseverance. He went on to become a great sales executive. To some, working more than what is productive is a waste of resources. A 2.1 GPA student works to graduate. What good is it to spend time on "fluff" when the object is to focus on what they need to learn and obtain their degrees. This efficiency is characteristic of many successful business people.

Perfection is a wonderful thing, but small business is about a series of judgments on how to allocate precious resources. Getting a 2.1 on cleaning the break room is a lot less important than getting a 4.0 on customer service. Not all things are equal, nor should they be given the same weight. The successful business person cannot afford perfection in all things. Sometimes "just enough" is the optimum.

In "*Outliers*," Malcolm Gladwell illustrates how basketball success is not increased by height over a certain amount. Most will acknowledge that being 5'4" is a major hindrance to a professional basketball career. On the other hand, being 7'6'' does not ensure being the best. You simply need to be <u>tall enough</u>, say 6'4." Michael Jordan, the greatest player, was 6'6" tall.[27]

In business, the millionaires are all smart enough. Some have more intellect than necessary, but extra intellect does not increase the chances of success. Values and character are much more important, and tie more directly to success than does intellect.

A few key observations in Stanley's work shed valuable light onto the important issue of values to becoming a business millionaire. Here are the top five characteristics, listed by millionaires themselves:

- Integrity –being honest with people
- Discipline—applying self-control
- Social skills—getting along with people
- A supportive spouse
- Hard work—more than most people

I doubt that all these people read or were influenced by Napoleon Hill's "*Think and Grow Rich*" of 1937 but the list sounds very much like Hill's famous writings, as well as Andrew Carnegie and other ultra-successful business people in history. Only "a supportive spouse" may have been missing, but of course, a century ago this was simply a common expectation of family life. Perhaps it is mentioned now because otherwise we might assume strong families no longer influence success. Clearly and emphatically wrong! (Here is perhaps the time to state that about 30% of business startups are now headed by women; those women often have strong, supportive husbands. When the business grows sufficiently, the husband may work for the wife in a compatible, supportive role.)

This is quite a different evaluation than the general public and press have of business owners. But it is completely congruent with my decades of working directly with these kinds of successful businesses. The successful business owners rate from high to stellar in each of these

> **During the Great Recession of 2009 it was not uncommon for small business owners to put money into the business to cover losses in order to keep cherished employees. They rarely tell the employees what happened; they do it out of compassion.**

characteristics: integrity clearly being number one. These businessmen believe deeply in what used to be American standards for honor.

Unlike impersonal Wall Street, big business, quasi-governmental agencies and financial institutions, the successful small business people I have been in contact with for over 30 years rarely exhibit failures in what we used to call "American Values." They are, regardless of religious persuasion, strong representatives of what is good in people in America. They care about people, provide jobs that pay as much as they can afford, and strive to be ethical. These characteristics show through in customers' attitudes about these businesses, and it speaks volumes about how we should go forward as a country.

Perhaps this is why they are successful. Consumers and journalists are quick to condemn business fraud, abysmal customer services, and cheating by businesses. Unscrupulous businesses, as Chapter 6 on PIMS made clear, are not rewarded by customers; they have their margins squeezed, and remain mediocre or ultimately die. Ethics do play a part in success, and those who become millionaires share high ethical standards. Are they successful because of high ethics or are high ethics required to become successful? In any case, high ethical standards strongly correlate to success and clearly must be a part of successful business practices. It would be better if all businesses were highly ethical. Meanwhile, those that succeed usually are.

The Keys To The Kingdom

Perhaps the most important of Stanley's research findings is this:

> [M]ost millionaires saw an opportunity that others ignored, and had willingness to take financial risk given the promise of a good and rational return.... Investing in themselves, it appears to them, is a much better risk than the stock market or other get rich quick schemes.

Stanley paraphrases what millionaires say about themselves: "[W]e provide a product or service that has strong demand but few suppliers to fulfill that demand. We do not follow the crowd."[28]

Extraordinary! Across various industries the people who become millionaires have somehow selected products and services in a niche market with little competition. They found a crack in the market. The same confidence that allows them to dispense with worrying about academic grades, with the intelligence and drive to achieve, also enables them to see society in a way to discover cracks, and to think they can succeed at what most fail at.

These folks were not all brilliant MBA's. Indeed, they have studied varied subjects and may have no MBA. Yet somehow—because of natural instinct, or conscious thinking, or by sheer luck—they selected a crack in the market that allowed their business to flourish. They flourish, according to the axioms of PIMS, with or without strong management skills, or great marketing prowess.

> **Luck plus smarts, hard work, ethical corporate behavior and being well positioned in your niche markets are the essence of small business success.**

Where does this entrepreneurial spirit, self-confidence and drive come from? One could argue that a well-rounded, socially adept, broad thinker is actually better than a "smart" person at seeing the universe. I don't think the data necessarily supports this, because we are only examining the winners, the millionaires—and not the many thousands of losers.

We probably <u>can</u> say that entrepreneurs who select a good prospective crack in a market will have a better chance of growing and keeping the business. In addition, good management skills, people skill, and reasonable intelligence will increase the chances of successfully competing. Moreover, the chance of success in capturing a niche market are substantially increased when there is a narrow focus from an operational perspective and little or no competition. Those odds are further enhanced for people who opt for a fiscally conservative lifestyle, creating a cushion for financial trouble.

And finally, customers will reward a business they perceive to be ethical, honest and marked by integrity. These are the elements of success; the list of "must have characteristics" for small business success. It is clearly possible to fail while possessing all these characteristics, but when these characteristics are not present failure is nearly assured.

Way down the list of key characteristics Stanley discovered was luck. Millionaires placed this as number 27 of the top characteristics. I understand why they would do so, but think luck is more important than that. Undoubtedly many people did everything exactly the same as the millionaires with one exception. Perhaps they missed the crack in the market, or the market changed in a way that could not have been anticipated or expected. No one can predict developments in the economy or from technical change.

Could TomTom (GIS mapping for your car) have imagined that all smart phones would have free powerful GIS? Should Yahoo, Microsoft or hundreds of other search engines have known what Google would do to search processes in 1998? How many of our gurus really anticipated the deep real estate depression of 2008? How many of the millionaires polled in Stanley's research are flat broke today because they were in real estate? Yes, luck plays a very real part of success.

Being lucky and smart, being well positioned in your niche markets, plus hard work and ethical corporate behavior are the essence of small business success. When these factors occur, success increases dramatically, even with poor management, weak planning and minimal marketing. In my early retail career I demonstrated a talent for a specific market at a specific time. Yet, luck was very important to my success. When fashion changed, our luck (and unique niche) had run out.

"If people want what you have, they will beat a path to your door to get it." Don Griffith Jr.

Chapter Post Script

Upon publishing of this book, another was released called *The Triple Package: How three unlikely traits explain the rise and fall of cultural groups in America*, by Amy Chua and Jed Rubenfeld. The book looks at research on the most successful groups, which turn out to be cultural subgroups in the U.S.. Highly successful people tend to cluster in these groups.

They conclude that the "triple package," the three characteristics that the individuals have, formed by the culture they grow up in, create a combination of drive and delayed gratification necessary to succeed. This well researched book strongly supports research and observation I have cited above.

Chapter 9   Matching Core Competencies with Market Cracks

Until now, I have not defined marketing. Having looked at several text books, researchers, respected authors and decades of field work, here is my definition of marketing: it is the "process" of matching company *core competencies to customer wants and needs*. Simple. Elegant. Notice I don't mention price promotions, sales or any of the other dozen or so *activities* that fall under this definition. These activities implement, accomplish and enhance the definition, so are a part of the marketing process—but not marketing per se.

"Process" is key here. **Marketing is not a department any more than "management" is a department**! It's true that managers try to departmentalize most functions, but marketing cuts across most if not all departments, just as the process of managing does. It cannot and should not be departmentalized. Remember the definition of marketing? Matching your competencies to customers' wants. To accomplish this requires research, engineering, production, customer service, promotion and innovation. Legend Professor, Peter Drucker's dictum: "Businesses exist to create a customer and innovate".[29] Marketing is the innovation process that creates new niches, and the communication of a product's value. Does this sound like a single department? Furthermore, most small companies don't have, and can't afford, an executive level decision maker responsible for marketing. Yet everything you have learned so far clearly puts the responsibility at the ownership or top management level.

As David Packard, founder of Hewlett Packard, put it, "Marketing is too important for marketing people to do." If he meant the people in the marketing department, I agree. Owners are the chief strategic marketers. People in the executive suites are the ones responsible for setting strategic direction. They must understand the core competencies of the organization, technology, labor, marketing channels and partners, financial assets and creative innovation. They need to understand all this in order to match these factors with their best customers, with customers' wants, needs, desires, requirements, demands, whims, and financial capabilities.

Owners and top managers who believe their marketing people can sell whatever is in the warehouse are assigning a difficult task, rarely achieved satisfactorily. This unrealistic expectation is what gives marketers a sleazy reputation. It probably accounts for the fact that C\chief marketing officers at large companies last only an average of 22 months. The truth is, the president is responsible for selecting marketing strategy. He or she may have help from the CMO, CFO, etc. to analyze all the moving parts required to properly position the company and its primary products. Nonetheless, it is the president who signs off. It is just too convenient for the president to fire the CMO for being unable to sell what the company has in the warehouse. This is a common issue and a fundamental error of owners and presidents.

As you can see, considerable evidence illustrates that companies that are well emplaced in their markets do well. Seldom, if ever, does one person (the top marketing person) create success simply by making an emplacement or positioning decision. The entire company must do so, because the process of marketing involves everyone up and down every branch of the organizational chart.

Small companies that succeed seem to do so primarily because they serve their market cracks well. The owners or CEO could see where the opportunity was, and worked to align the company to fill that crack. Looking at the diverse profile of people who are successful business owners reveals they do have at least this one attribute in common.

Not so long ago, I was called in by a consulting friend to review a company's "marketing ideas." This 60 year old company produced luxury furniture; so the recession, I reasoned, must have caused reduced sales. But the situation was more dire than that: employees were fighting internally about who was responsible for marketing. They had used up all their cash and unwisely expanded two years before. Sales volume had dropped nearly 60 percent in just three years. The recession had much to do with the large drop. Cheap imports from China were another big factor. The perfect storm was completed when they managed to lose the strong sales team they once had. The company had no sales force, down from 14 people two years before. This was a company on the brink of bankruptcy.

We spent a couple of hours touring the factory and show rooms, and hearing about the new marketing ideas to generate more sales. It felt like they were rearranging the deck chairs on the sinking Titanic! The company needed complete re-positioning to regain old customers, yet they were thinking about new promotions. This company clearly had competencies. They had factories, skilled woodworkers, very savvy designers who created innovative game furniture. But somehow they had become disconnected from their customers. The old relationship between competency and customers was nearly gone.

New promotional ideas may help, but 60 percent of the volume will not be created based on last minute promotions. This company must reposition itself into a new crack. To do so, the people, working together, must evaluate where the market is, and then set out to fill that market with products that their customers want at prices they can afford. This can be difficult when we pay ten times more for workers here than we do for off-shore production. Strategies do exist to remedy this problem. But the strategies start at core competencies and customers, not the marketing promotion level. This company failed to watch customers so that it could maintain its crack in the market. It failed to understand its value diamond. As we have seen, high price can be created. Starbucks and Polo have done precisely this. But this furniture company had not created appropriate value and brand for its dealers and customers. The former sales department was simply trying to sell the same old standby winners—at three times the price of the competing Chinese products. An internal marketing department would have done no better.

The owners were guilty of running a sales department without a positioning strategy. They certainly lacked a marketing *process*.

What Does Competency Look Like?

Dictionary.com defines competence as "adequacy: possession of required skill, knowledge, qualification or capacity." Simple enough, perhaps. When applied to beating your competition, however, possessing adequate or qualified ability or knowledge is insufficient, unless, of course, you define what is being produced much more narrowly. Brithinee Electric is certainly competent, but so are most of its competitors. However, when Brithinee's specific crack is defined as "repairs to the highest standards available," this company can separate itself from the others in a very technical way—a "small crack in the market" way.

"Only Brithinee Electric can deliver Brithinee Quality" is one of the company's branding and differentiating statements. This is not only a statement, however. It is supported by real explanation of standards, materials, techniques and the performance of the repairs. Positioning Brithinee Electric as the highest quality, in this market, translates to longer use and therefore better use of capital for the buyer. Yes, its services are more expensive than those of almost all of their competitors; but they cater to users of large motors mission critical processes or difficult to remove generators such as wind generators. The differentiation is supported by three internal PhD's who love working on the technical aspects of exactly why their materials and techniques are higher quality.

So back to competency — Brithinee Electric's market crack is not "any" motor repair. This crack is for a motor or generator in special circumstances: difficult to replace, or very heavy use. The motor owner wants a longer motor life and higher efficiency. Not all large motors fit this particular market crack. If they don't, a new motor may be a better solution. But this crack is large enough to keep the motor repair business growing in a mature market, during a recession. Not bad work!

In this case, competency includes not only the high level of workmanship, but extremely deep knowledge of the materials used to rewind a motor. Having carefully researched various materials for many years, and given their special interest in building the very best motor rewind, Brithinee personnel have learned how to reduce failures to perhaps the lowest in the world, nearly approaching zero.

The above is an example of technical competency. Matching this competency to the customer requires a sophisticated customer who understands this level of competency. Marketing communications is the function that bridges any gaps between sophistication and technical competency.

Systems Technology Inc. has a unique competency in building post-printing machines that handle high volumes of paper. Publishers of newspapers and magazines must be able to handle enormous quantities of finished product to keep the high speed web printers going. Systems Technology has built a variety of machinery to fold, stack, collate, turn, and bundle these products.

Long before the Great Recession of 2009, the printing industry was in decline. Then the recession nearly choked all investment out of the industry. This became a perfect storm for John St. John, Systems Technology's president. But he knew the company had a deep core competency in how to handle, monitor, and control huge numbers of objects. Systems Technology now needed a new crack in which to apply its core competencies. It turned out that with a simple adaption to handle small boxes instead of stacks of paper, Systems Technology could excel in high speed packaging, addressing, sorting and stacking for shipment. The obvious use was to build sophisticated "manufacturing" lines for handling products upon completion, or that are pulled from inventory to ship.

This can be a complex issue for large fulfillment companies with traditional catalog operations, or that have grown out of the huge Internet shopping-cart business. Multiple items must be gathered for shipment into a single box. Millions of addresses must be sent to variable data printers, and joined up to the right box. Then the shipment must be verified by both weighing the box and checking the address again to make sure it matches. Any box marked incorrectly is kicked off the conveyer belt. Finally the shipping manifest must be printed and/or prepared to coordinate data with the shipping company.

This is a unique marriage of mechanical engineering, photo recognition, software programming and packaging knowledge. So STI is building a completely new niche market, one that allows the automated shipping of over 20 packages a minute. The market exists, even if only some warehouses need this volume and STI intends to fill the small crack. The problem? Not the technology. It's communicating to prospects the cost savings of using accurate machines instead of human hands likely to make mistakes.

Brithinee Electric and Systems Technology are examples of deep and specific core competencies. They are difficult to emulate or copy. Many companies try to succeed in a customer service competency. This is more fuzzy than most technical competencies. Almost every company thinks it excels in customer service. Most smaller companies have an easier time tracking down problems and think this is the solution. Moreover, many smaller companies think that this is enough to justify a higher price. This is not, however, the whole story; in reality, the customer does not "perceive" much difference.

Customer service must be stellar to be noticed. It is not confined to answering the phone and solving problems. It must be looked at from the prospecting stage all the way through the post-sale stage. And the WOW factor should be part of the innovation process of the company. Innovation is not reserved for product development. Customer service also needs innovation and help.

Great customer service includes solving customer problems or even designing customer products. A plastic injection molding company was engaged to solve problems in developing a new template mapping the brain; this would help in some very precise brain surgery to relieve symptoms of Parkinson's disease. Only a dozen surgeons were well trained enough to perform the surgery. They thought that if they could design a cranial cap template to guide placement of the probes, they could train other surgeons more quickly.

Drawing a complex three dimensional product is one thing. Casting it is entirely another. The plastic company pulled their engineering people together to solve the technical problems and helped complete the final design. This, too, is a form of customer service.

Customer service includes purchasing assistance, shipping services, engineering and technical services, online efficiencies, follow up checks, satisfaction surveys, social media, and an infinite number of other new ideas. Many others have already written good works on customer service: this is not my purpose here. But you need to see how customer service is a marketing function — part of the marketing process. **Customer service is a necessary differentiator and a competency that is part of solving the positioning problem and creating value.**

Competency includes standard business practices as well. In some businesses, financial competency is part of the product. Cars, motor homes and real estate require financial competency as a deliverable. Banking should as well, although lately one might wonder if they have any lending competencies. Financial stability is a competency in many kinds of companies where long life of product or service is needed. Few companies sell this as a benefit.

A grand old home, down the street from mine, finally succumbed to the occasional rains of Southern California. From the street, the roof of the two-story Spanish Colonial looked like red tile. But a closer look revealed that it was really formed tin. During its 98 years, one of the owners had the roof painted a reddish clay color. Now it finally needed repairs.

Using the Internet, only a few companies fit the description. The home owner first called a manufacturer in St. Louis. The home owner described the roofing material. The alert customer service person asked for the city and address, then replied, "Sir, we manufactured your roof some 98 years ago. I'm so sorry. The warrantee was only good for 95 years. But we do have the original tin forms if you need more tiles."

Naturally the owner didn't expect a warrantee. But, using the original tiles on a now historic building secured the $65,000 replacement roof sale with a new 95 year warrantee. The value is apparent. This is an example of customer service as a market differentiator.

Remember the company with Acme Duplex spring balances for double hung windows? Popular in the 1930s and 1940s, they replaced the old rope and weight balances. Using the Internet a company now can "get found" based on a few trademarked brands for the original product.

Both of these companies are examples where the crack is so small that others have trouble competing. They have survived for a century, a feat very few can boast about. Today, they use their distinct competences and longevity and U.S. built quality to maintain control of their markets.

Assess your company's assets and competencies, because it is literally what you have to sell. It's the ability to create new products or efficiently manufacture a product, as well as the uniqueness of the product itself. Marketing and management, brain trusts, and people who are good at what they do produce competencies. In fact, finding the right people for the job is a competency that solves the lack of competency.

Think of your competencies as a set of skills and assets that can be assembled into a variety of projects, services, products, and designs, always looking for re-formation to adapt to customers' ever-changing needs and wants.

Chapter 10   Positioning Your Company In A Crack In The Market

Of all the fields in the marketing process, marketing positioning and emplacement are the most important. Interestingly, of the powerful gurus who write about marketing, a few dominate the thought on positioning. These are Jack Trout, Al Ries, and Steve Rivkin. (All the books by these three are worthwhile reading following this book.)

They generally define positioning as "a system for finding a window in the market or more specifically the <u>consumer mind.</u>"[30] Ries specifically states on his web site, "Positioning is not what you do to the product; it's what you do to the mind of the prospect. It's how you differentiate your brand in the mind. Positioning compensates for our over communicated society by using an oversimplified message to cut through the clutter and get into the mind. **Positioning focuses on the perceptions of the prospect not on the reality of the brand.**"[31]

Ries emphasizes developing "perceptions." Indeed this is an important part of how small businesses must position services and products. But I believe small companies can much more materially position themselves in a physical way, innovative way, and more strategic way.

Market Emplacement is only slightly different. I define emplacement as **the process of placing your company between your customers and your competition.** This is in a more physical and less mental sense. The smaller your niche, the fewer competitors you will likely have. The more competitors you have, the tougher it is to "protect" your customers. This can be done with products within your niche market as well. Add the mental positioning of the customer mind and the differentiation can be realized.

The positioning experts have spent decades studying large businesses with heavy competition in the middle of the market share range (#4 in market share down through the low price leader). In addition to creating a perception in the mind, creating a real micro-market niche and shutting out the competition is where the profit performance is. In my Value Diamond, image (along with quality and service) is the component best used to create the "mental" part of value. I think Trout, Ries and Rivkin will agree with my extension of positioning into the value diamond. If they do, they can explain how millionaires exist in basic industries like trash hauling, plumbing, dentistry, and independent convenience stores.

Emplacement

Imagine a chess board set up with white pieces on one side and black on the other. The white chess pieces represent customers. The black ones are competitors. The space in between these two groups is the competitive landscape. The competitors are carefully examining your customers on the other side, figuring out ways to take them away from you. Your company is in this space, trying to keep competitors away from your customers. (Customers here can also be prospective customers.)

Now, imagine your blocking strategy as a playing card, and hold it on its side in between your customers and competitors.

If you place the card so it is very close to a group of the competition, *several* of the competitor playing pieces will be unable to see *any* of your customers; but the remaining will. If you place your card close to your customers, not all will be protected, but a *few* will be unseen by *nearly all* competitors.

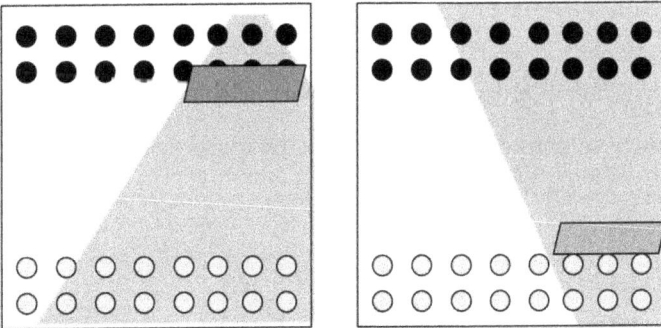

Figure 5: The left chess board seeks to protect many customers (grey pieces) from a few competitors, while the right seeks to protect a few valued customers from most competitors.

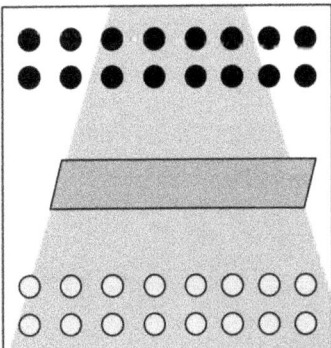

Figure 6: A dominant company has a foot print larger than a normal playing card and can block most competitors from seeing any customers.

159

So the task at hand is to determine where the best emplacement on the board is to best protect your customers. It could be argued that keeping the king and queen from seeing any customers leaves your company the best opportunity to protect all customers from the remaining playing pieces. But it can also be argued that if you really know your customers, you will pick the most valuable ones and stay close to them, so none of the competitive players even know they exist.

Relationship marketing works where the continual transaction and very tight relationship with customers creates a trust so strong, that no competitor will ever have a chance to take a customer (if they even become aware of them).

Now think of your customers as a somewhat diverse group, just like the chess pieces. If you can align your highest value customers on one end of the board, you can block most competition from seeing them. Likewise, imagine that your competition is diverse and may move from one square to another, or even come closer to your customers. This represents the constant movement of the market place.

If possible, you would try to dominate the market. This is like having a playing card that can be any size you like or expands as large as possible. A manila folder sized card would protect most customers from most competitors. A competitor would have to become very creative to "see" your customers, let alone steal them.

Market emplacement and positioning your company probably have more to do with the success of your marketing than any other activity that follows.

What are the aspects of the location and size of the card? This is a combination of core competencies, differentiation of product, brand, and perceived value.

An example might be a gas station that offers the only free car wash in the local geographic market. For those drivers who really must have a clean car, this "extra" (assuming price, quality, and service are the same) easily explains why you will keep customers. For that group who must have a clean car, the rest of the competition is not in consideration. The card has been made large and placed closer to customers. The ones on the end, who don't really care about washing their car, can, for other reasons, go across the street to the station that offered no free car wash. Further, if you had the magic ability to keep all competition from installing a car wash, you would dominate that local market niche. You may even get them to pay a premium for gas in order to get a free car wash.

This may be a good time to illustrate how government regulation influences natural markets. For those who are doing business with a gasoline re-imbursement, the bonus is a free, employer paid car wash, altering otherwise normal behavior because the employer can create a tax free expense. Very small alterations in government policy can easily open up or eliminate small niche markets, making changes in government policies an unfair competitive influence. I was astonished to hear Barnard Marcus, a founder of Home Depot, once say on John Stossel's show, "We could not start our business today based on the new regulations. Of course, in a way, we shouldn't complain because it is so difficult now that we won't see any competitors in our market." He went on to say that we can afford the highly paid professionals to interpret and mitigate all the regulations. We could not have afforded this when we were starting. In this situation, an existing market is preserved simply by over-regulation.

We are all familiar with loyalty programs and frequent purchase programs; these seek to create greater perceived value, leading to the preferences for a customer to return to their airline, restaurant, or store. These are attempts at market emplacement. The most direct way to emplace your company, or find a small niche market, is to focus on the customers' wants, needs and desires, and to deliver greater **perceived value**.

The goal is to provide the best value for the specific niche for the specific target prospects, in their language. Language includes the subtleties of each profession, industry, demographic cohort. It includes aesthetic and cultural "language." Understanding the intricacies of positioning requires some discussion of the various elements: customers, competitors, product differentiation, brand and value.

Customers

Many businesses take their customers for granted. Oh, they think they know them because they talk to them when they order, or review the sales etc. Unfortunately, I very rarely work with a new client who knows everything necessary to know about the client's customers.

Businesses do have a range of touch points between customers, so I will need to generalize. If you sell movie tickets or hot dogs, you are in a very transactional business. Customers want to exchange money for the experience or tangible product. You can only infer information about customers from other information. If you are an accountant serving a business, or you supply products to retailers, you will tend to have a string of transactions that can develop into a relationship. Relationships occur between companies, as well as among people within companies. Both of these types are useful. But we want to create data that is useful to understand the nature of the customer.

One of the first dimensions to examine is the relationship between size of customer revenue and customer rank. As straight forward as this seems, gathering (and then examining) a year's worth of data is not always easy. Fortunately, today's inexpensive accounting programs makes this much easier than it used to be.

Most companies experience Pareto's Principle, or "The 80-20 Rule." This states that 80 percent of the effects come from 20 percent of the transactions or events. In other words, 80 percent of your revenue will come from 20 percent of your customers.

This remarkable concept holds true for most of my analyses of customer revenue. It does range higher and lower. As high as 95 percent and as low as 60 percent of your revenue can be generated by 20 percent of your customers. In any case, the consequence is that companies at the high level (or even at 80 percent) can lose substantial revenue with each good customer they lose. Those with a low ratio have the luxury of a broader customer mix, where each customer is less valuable to the total.

Revenue is one thing; but profit is a better measure. Re-evaluating your top customers by profit (or gross margin) normally creates a different set in the top 20 percent. When this happens, it dramatically illustrates that some customers have greater costs associated with them than others. Your "best" customers are the ones producing the highest margins, right?

An even better measure is the contribution margin. High volume customers might not produce the highest profit, but they produce enough dollar margin to cover a substantial part of your fixed costs. If the company is not to lose money, the loss of one huge customer with a lower margin can increase the contribution required by all remaining customers of fixed costs.

Knowing which customers make up the top 10, 20 and 50 percent of the revenue contribution creates an actionable promotional opportunity. Using a specific promotional campaign to pull more customers into the top 10 percent can boost business rapidly, and perhaps show that you appreciate those customers more. Adding more customers to the top 50 percent normally is a different type of campaign. Of course, asking the bottom to leave, or exposing the bottom customers to your competitors can cut the expenses required to support low revenue customers. Sometimes, leaving the bottom customers (perhaps they are very far away, or their "issues" take up a disproportionate amount of your time) for your competition to deal with is a smart tactic.

Another form of the Pareto's Principle approach can be made using gross margin and net profit. Comparing the top revenue customers with the top profit customers can yield a disappointing result when the largest revenue customers fall into the mid-range of margin and profit. These are big gorilla customers: the ones who demand discounts and special service because of their buying power. This necessarily takes resources from your most profitable customers, thereby risking lower customer service performance. The marketing event or action for this circumstance is entirely different from the previous scenarios.

Within this general report format is much more information. Do the same report for each division, product group and product to reveal the breadth of engagement with your big customers across product lines. Maintaining this business is one campaign, while extending breadth with those customers with just a few products or lines is another type. Each "campaign" addresses a specific targeted group with a specific goal, requiring specific language to communicate value to that group. This is the simplicity of serving a small crack in the market. Specific needs can be more easily communicated. General needs (large niches) or mass marketing are much more difficult to communicate and naturally come with a larger cost.

Other information besides revenue and margin data should be captured for further analysis. Understanding seasonal trends, sporadic behavior, the decision makers, and their personal profiles, buying motivations and other competing vendors is valuable as well. The goal is to learn how to communicate effectively with each decision maker and influencer, in order to demonstrate value. Armed with this information and a clear-cut value proposition, writing copy, image creation and marketing tactics become easier. No heroic advertising or promotional efforts are necessary: just tell your story in a professional way, based on intimate knowledge and a strong relationship with your customers.

When a company is positioned well, the content development is easier to create.

Competitors

Determining the range of your competitors seems like a daunting task for a small business. It may seem less so, however, when you remember that your niche in the market should be defined as the <u>smaller</u> niche that you <u>actually serve</u>, rather than the <u>market you dream about</u> expanding into. Many small businesses advertise to a much larger area than they actually serve. They hope to grow geographically rather than become more relevant where they are. This broad advertising can drain your ability to serve your real niche.

Business to Business

Most business-to-business owners know who beats them occasionally on which bid. You learn this from prospects looking for your product. If this is not the case, look in the yellow pages in your primary business category. Alternatively, Google your business category and business geography to see who shows up. Cross reference these methods and you have a starting point with several main business competitors.

Study these companies' websites carefully to determine how much direct competition they really are. Finally, use an online list service such as InfoUSA.com® to look up these businesses. When you buy the full information on them, you will have a good idea of their revenue size, number of employees, locations of facilities, key employees and more. Collect the information in a spreadsheet with your information in one row. Pay special attention to the primary services and products offered on the website and compare with your own.

Now think about your customers and ask yourself whether your competition has similar types of customers. Chances are that some of these competitors are different enough to remove them from your main competition list. Compare this value proposition using the Burgess Value Diamond in Chapter 7.

Business to Consumers

Businesses serving consumers normally have a more complex set of customer types. Creating relationships can be challenging in industries where customers simply want a transaction (like buying a hot dog). But data is still valuable in order to understand more about your business. The 80-20 rule is also useful in examining products and service revenue categories. List the revenue volume by product in order to compare the top products or services to the marginal ones. Look at gross profit in the same way, comparing the two lists against each other.

Many businesses invest in products that weigh down their inventory because they take too long to sell. Retail and wholesale businesses need computerized inventory systems to track these items properly. Proper turnover of inventory is also essential because investment can be tied up too long with unrecognized slow movers. The PIMS principles indicate that capital investment can lower the profitability of second tier market leadership. Inventory dysfunction is the number one culprit for retail failures: Retailers and wholesalers must become experts in this area to survive and grow.

Your inventory analysis is a good way to learn who your customers are—and thus to defining your crack in the market. Your customers all have buying behaviors. They make decisions based first on value; but what they buy is an interesting dance of behaviors, based on age, income, education and culture, upbringing and economic conditions. Consumer behavior is a complex subject on which millions of business dollars are spent every year. Modern researchers are watching cameras to detect what cereal boxes are looked at, examined and finally purchased. They use brain scans to determine when real pleasure areas are excited by wine consumption of various labels. One reason this is so important to marketers is that consumers do not really understand their own behavior, making surveys suspect.

Smaller businesses cannot afford most of the expensive research that is done by larger businesses. But much of this research is available, after the fact, for several hundred dollars through the research company websites, or press releases that researchers use to publicize the completion of the study.

Other affordable ways of achieving similar understanding for your products (here "products" also refers to services that are purchased) are available using both demographic information and psychographic or life-style information. Using the names and addresses of your customers, you can append the list with additional data that describes their demographic profile and lifestyle, or buy profiles.

Psychographics

Also called life-style data, psychographic information seeks to explain more than demographic data. Three primary systems are in use. Each system divides all U.S. consumers into between 50 and 75 groups. Each segment includes households with similar life-style choices and buying behaviors. While similar life-styles have a range of ages and other demographics, the ranges rarely represent a mirror of the population as a whole.

For instance, high income households may be divided into six or eight segments. The very highest income group is generally older than the other high income segments because money is accumulated during life. Nonetheless, all segments contain mixes of race, age groups, and religions. What each group usually has in common is taste and consumption pattern, as seen in the type of neighborhood they live in, the cars they drive, the news they consume, their educational level, and the kind of vacations they take. Each attribute has a range, but the ranges are much narrower than for the population as a whole.

The full range of segments generally, but not always, goes from low income to high income. Upper middle income households, for instance, can include those who are fiscally conservative, live in middle class neighborhoods, and drive Fords. At the other end of the spectrum, some households stretch too far to buy a home above their means, and own BMW's and power boats. Despite identical income, education and age, these two segments are different.

Psychographic analysis can clarify family values. "First adopters" tend to want new things: the latest fashions, new high tech phones, and TV's. Meanwhile, more conservative folks buy only when the price drops and they see a monetary value that makes sense in the context of their conservative lifestyle. This is just one dimension, but already you can see the relative tendency (again, it is not more than that) of the fashion-forward and early adopters to act spontaneously and to overspend. If you are in fashion retailing, this is a good customer. If you are a banker making car loans, on the other hand, you prefer the conservative family making a high down payment because they want to pay off the loan quickly.

Knowing what mix of these life-style segments your customers are in is extremely helpful in order to match your core competencies with your customer mix. Knowing who your customers are, or who buys and appreciates your products, is proof of your core competencies. I measure core competency in this way: what you sell profitably is in fact what your customers want and what identifies your core competency.

Home furnishing retailers who don't understand the difference between these two groups will struggle. The Mercedes owner segment will buy home furnishings based on the style, prestige, and brand and will be less concerned about the price. With this group, being able to afford it is sometimes the fulfillment as much as the object itself. In contrast, Ford owners are more practical and will only buy when they have a real need. To them, perceived quality means it will last longer. They may buy a high end lamp; but they will see value in the material quality, longevity and good deal.

So which group will your company cater to? Can it be both? The answer is yes — but. Because the Mercedes segment is the front edge of fashion (or early adopters), the Ford buyer is the back end. One buys immediately; the others love a sale and will buy only when they have gotten used to the new styles and value the lower price. A ready-to-wear retailer can sell new goods to the fashion-forward household and then put items on sale for the fashion laggard. But the cycle for furniture may be too long to wait for the sale. In this case, the furniture store must cater to the optimal customer segments.

A retail store buyer must have discriminating taste to buy properly. Anticipation of the buying habits of the fickle, fashion-forward segments can be a real crap shoot.

I live in a smaller, traditional town in Southern California. The residents include a segment of high asset, upper middle class income households. Because our town offers a very high level of well attended cultural activities, many independent retailers are fooled into thinking that they will cater to the "rich" (in their eyes) customers in town. But no high-end retailer ever succeeds. First, the proportion of fashion-forward households to traditional, conservative households is very small. Second, those who want the latest are willing to drive an hour into L.A., Orange County or Palm Desert to shop, so they can tell their friends where they bought it.

In my town, therefore, the high end store is doomed from the start. Large retailers don't make this mistake, because they use life-style data for careful location analysis. Local developers wanted Nordstrom to come to our little city, because the developers wanted the image. But Nordstrom turned us down, knowing we don't have enough of their best customers to be successful.

Who do you serve?

Life-style segmentation can also help you understand personal services, media consumption, political persuasion and investment strategy. Our local banks thrive, because this is a community of savers and investors, not high-end consumers. One successfully demonstrated strategy was to start a bank in town to collect the money, and then open branches in other cities where they could loan the money.

You prove your ability to serve certain segments when you append your own customer list with data from one of the life-style data sets. It helps you to better define your target customers. If you have mostly middle income customers, you will price yourself out of the market if you buy merchandise that is too expensive. What you sell now, and who you sell it to, *already defines your core competencies*. If you only sell occasionally to a particular customer type, that fact says something about your product mix, breadth of your category, or your customer service.

Another valuable use of data is to determine the market size. When you know your top five lifestyle segments, you can get a count (and the addresses) of those five segments within your market area. By estimating how much of their income might be spent on your merchandise, you can calculate roughly how much total revenue will be generated by these customers. Comparing that number to your revenue says volumes about your success and your competitor's success. It also serves as a guide to buying price points, quality levels and styles to cater to that set of customers, while properly balancing your inventory. (Do not buy inventory for segments that you are not serving well.)

The available sales dollars that you are not getting are most likely spent with competitors or in an adjacent geographic market area. For example, say your bike business is already at $550,000 and you think the market for bicycle repairs is $600,000. You will stop growing soon, and don't need to expand. If the market is $3,000,000 then you have room to grow; meanwhile, lots of business is going somewhere else. Now you can put your competitive analysis against the market and build a plan to capture more sales and fill more of your crack in the market.

The discussion above is a way to illustrate the information that is useful to position your company appropriately in your crack in the market. It is not exhaustive in any way. My bibliography in the appendix, lists several books useful to understanding of business and customers. However, some skills and sense of the market are always required to interpret the data. Luckily, consultants exist to help with these specialized strategic issues. In addition, you can use the Internet to find resources in the area of customers and competition.

Use your internal data and buy external data to understand your customers. An old business consulting friend, John Haythe, often said, "Mind your own business, and mind it well." If you pay attention to what your numbers are telling you, you'll better understand your crack in the market.

Chapter 11   More on Emplacing Your Company In Your Crack In The Market

Let's re-visit our emplacement chessboard to reconsider the customer side and the competitive side. Your goal is to block your best customers from your toughest competitors' ability to "see" them. You have carefully examined your customers and know as much as possible about them. You have also narrowed your list to a few, more direct competitors.

You know from Chapter 6 that you will profit most if your customers consider you to be higher in quality and service. You know that if you lead your market niche, you will be rewarded by your customers more than if you are number four or below. If you are in the top three, you get a larger "competency card" than a regular playing card. It is much easier to block competitors if you are a front runner because you have a larger footprint, or larger market share which creates more financial resources.

Leadership in the market has its distinct advantages. Al Ries says in *Focus—The Future of Your Company Depends on It* that leading companies attract more and better employees. They have the first crack at distribution; they have the money for innovation and marketing. Perhaps most powerfully, you can't get into trouble if you buy from the leader in the market.[32] When you have a leadership place in your market you get a larger "card" to block with.

So now arrange your best customers in a cluster and move your company "card" so that you block your most important and dangerous competitors. Note that you can be more effective in blocking more of your important customers from your dreaded competitors. This shows how narrow your real crack in the market can be. When you create very narrow niches your large competitors have more problems watching your market carefully. Occupying your niche well has its advantages. This is the reverse of product or brand extension. It is a micro-niche approach to specific competencies, for specific customers, and for screening specific competitors.

Some of you are thinking, "But this is just part of my business. I need the rest, too and I can't cover all of my niches." An astute observation! Yes, protecting several small hairline cracks in your market simultaneously is difficult. Yet, this is the principle that keeps your large competitors from competing head-to-head with you. And if you want to maintain several cracks in the market, you need the resources to do it. Size and particularly breadth makes this harder. The exercise on the chess board may simplify the problem; but it is only an illustration. The more customers you want to screen, the more difficult a problem this becomes.

If you are trying to support a footprint/card that is too large or encompassing (all things to all customers), the following symptoms occur: poor customer service, less product knowledge, loss of customers, lower revenue per employee, and general loss of efficiency as your people and capital get stretched over more and more territory.

This is not unlike a battle where the enemy finds a way to flank your forces because you are defending too much territory with too few soldiers. Focusing on your market niche, on the other hand, eliminates areas of waste in your business. It's just like protecting a canon emplacement with a regiment: only overwhelming force can dislodge you. *Marketing Positioning* seeks to use differentiation to create perceived uniqueness. But the concept is also useful in discovering and "emplacing" your product or brand *intentionally* in your crack in the market.

Your Crack in the Market as an Economic Microcosm

Those of you who know something about economics have by now identified market cracks as a part of microeconomics (economics of companies and individuals). You are correct to think of the subject in this way. Supply and demand is very much in play in the success of smaller companies.

When we think of commodities (milk, wheat, coffee, copper, avocados, or thousands of products that we consume or are part of what we consume) we can't separate the supply from the demand. In a pure market economy, the price will fluctuate based on how much of the commodity is available compared with the demand for that product at any one time.

Avocado prices rise and fall based on how the current harvest is going and also on the current consumer demand. If consumers in the East catch up with the levels of taste for avocados in the West, the demand will increase, maintaining or increasing prices. Increasing prices provides an incentive for farmers to plant more trees, or for packers to invest in developing importing relationships with growers in other countries.

Thinking of the basic economics, this seems simple. And you may initially assume you cannot control or change anything about the free market economics of the issue. But economists also consider "substitution" and "elasticity" in the markets. When prices change, consumers may decide to substitute another fruit, buy another quality level, or buy different quantities.

While economists are aware that marketers try to differentiate, they don't always consider the power of branding on consumer demand. Although avocado prices have generally been increasing over the last decade, the California Avocado Commission, through its careful promotion of avocados, has helped to increase the average consumption per household. Contrast that to the orange market, where farmers in the U.S. have tough competition with imports. Supply is chasing demand, keeping prices low.

By focusing on the health, nutrition and taste of avocados, and expanding the "top of mind uses for avocados," the industry literally changed the demand curve based on external *perceptions* by customers. By increasing the value, compared with other fruits, consumers bought more, even as prices rose.

Of course, this little detail makes the neat supply/demand curve a little messier; but every[33] crack in the market behaves based on the laws of economics—even as marketers attempt to change that reality. This also illustrates that communications can influence demand even with commodities! Longmont Dairy has effectively done this with farm fresh milk delivered to the door step. The combination of high quality image and delivery creates an opportunity to sell milk for a premium despite its "commodity" category.

So imagine how products even more complex than avocados and milk can be effectively branded and differentiated to create more perceived value to the customer. Positioning your company and products, using differentiation from your competitors, is literally attempting to change the demand curve to your advantage by creating a perceived difference to the product in the customers' minds. Nor is the use of "perceived" in this case an attempt to say it is all smoke and mirrors. Rather this is to acknowledge that buyers do not make decisions based on facts alone. Emotion and perception also matter.

Even pragmatic, industrial engineers are not immune from perceptions. They buy based on company stability, what they believe the quality is, what they hear about others' beliefs in reliability or quality and sometimes, just because they have so many other decisions to make, they pick the easy choice. I know that scientific, accounting, engineering and financial experts think they are the typical "rational man." But every salesperson who works with them knows this is not true; it's just wishful thinking on their part.

It is all about perceptions and, when you read the section on "Aesthetics" later in this chapter, I think you will agree.

Your crack in the market functions as an economic model. Customers compare your products with your competitors' products and with replacement products, and even with regard to the importance in the market basket, given the budget available. It's worth the effort. The relationships of tens of millions of photographers, graphic artists, CPA's, engineers, personal services businesses, and many more create mini-markets based on personality or style.

So now let's take a closer look at how you can consider creating value to customers through differentiation and innovation.

How do you add value through differentiation?

Market differentiation of your company or product adds perceived value. As you assess your company against several competitors, using the Burgess Value Diamond, the degree to which you can create a perceived difference in quality, price, service or image is the degree to which you will stand out from the others.

Top thinkers on this illustrate these opportunities in a broader way:

- ♦ Increasing attributes of products (adding more apps to cell phones)

- Changing the attributes of products (color and design of laptops)
- Increasing the perceived quality (BMW's advanced handling)
- Creating a completely new product (Amazon's Kindle Reader)
- Adding convenience (banking in supermarkets)
- Providing better service (Nordstrom's)
- Standout packaging (the original Macintosh, the Kindle Fire)
- Extended variety (31 Flavors)
- Customization (ANCO hose couplings, Paramount Custom Wood Windows)
- Creating an experience (Starbucks)
- Faster turnaround (FedEx, Amazon)
- Strong brand (Polo)
- Aesthetics and design (Absolut Vodka and Disneyland)

You can use these differentiators, and many others, to set yourself apart from the competition. If you are in the top three in your crack, you have already done something that sets you apart. If you are in the middle, between the top three and the low cost producer, you need differentiation before you become irrelevant.

This *is* a tough job. Large companies spend millions on TQM (Total Quality Management) programs in an attempt to increase quality.

Unfortunately, of the tens of thousands of product innovations and new products developed every year, 95 percent or more fail.

If you are sandwiched in the middle, you need to carefully re-think your strategy to overcome your competitors. Having recently visited a business in trouble, I realized the only sensible solution was to abandon the old market crack and completely reinvent the company by moving to another crack where their existing core competencies could be used. They had dominated their crack for a half century, but imports and declining brand had eroded their ownership of the crack. This happens frequently, but lack of focus on the market crack allows others to slowly erode market share. Lack of management focus and agreement further eroded resources.

But the good news is that most small companies don't need to spend lots of TQM money. They simply need to understand their crack in the market better than anyone else. Add some creativity on top of that and you can be surprised by what you may accomplish. We tend to think that only people like Steve Jobs and Bill Gates can to this. Hogwash! I see small business owners and their creative people doing this all the time.

Here are some differentiators that made an impact on the overall value or brand of the company. All of these were small companies at one time.

Ray Kroc was a vendor to the McDonalds brothers in San Bernardino, California. He was impressed by the low cost and speed of service that they achieved in their walk-up hamburger restaurant. You know the rest of the story. McDonalds became a Fortune 500 company by creating a new paradigm — a new value footprint. The differentiators? Speed in service, convenience, and decent food at low prices.

Starbucks was started by creating a stronger, smoother coffee served in surroundings that changed the coffee shop business. The coffee was different and the environment created a different experience.

One of my motor repair business clients is alone in providing before and after photos on a report that details the problem and the suggested repair. The same company runs three shifts so essential motors can be repaired in as fast as three hours.

Mike Diamond sends "Smell Good Plumbers" to fix your broken plumbing. Having recognized that women who called the plumber did not want to smell the last job on the plumber, he made a simple procedural change that allowed him to advertise a powerful differentiator.

Amazon started by selling only books and music online. Book stores were late to the online sales game and are suffering greatly now.

Oxo Good Grips kitchenware built a whole new business by re-thinking how we grip utensils. By adding a larger, comfortable handle, they not only differentiated the design, they increased the comfort. Senior citizens with arthritis immediately saw the advantage of the better grip.[34]

Birkenstock made a sandal so ugly who would want to copy it? Over a long process of building a specific brand, based on appeal to counter-culture and the function of comfort, the company maintains a distinctive style that imitators can't replace.

Stew Leonard's Farm Fresh Foods markets have become legendary for home-town friendly service and innovation. Their five stores do the volume of ten competing stores. Initially, they differentiated themselves by having farm animals on the premises. Later they added innovative displays with animatronic animals, and a live petting zoo.

Modern Postcard distinguished themselves from other printers in a crowded, declining industry by making the highest quality, lowest priced and fastest delivery of post cards. Working from a high volume model enabled by new technology, the company captured millions of dollars by focusing on real differentiators.

Market Differentiation Elements

Here are some ideas to help you to explore differentiating your products and services. The best way to differentiate is to understand and target the elements that your *customers think* are important. Understanding your customers includes understanding their various kinds of expectations.

If your competitors are poor on service (many entire industries are poor on various elements in the Value Diamond), then you may have an opportunity to position your company differently in your crack in the market. If most are good on the phone and you are ok too, sending everyone to a telephone courtesy seminar may be an ineffective way to make a difference. This does not mean you don't want courtesy, it simply means other more difficult issues may have a higher priority. Business people understand that small businesses must carefully use all resources.

Changing the Attributes of Products

The mobile phone market today is a rapid growth market. The grandfather was the car phone, too big to carry around easily. In 1983, I thought it was amazing to call from the car. Today, teenagers think the mobile phone is more important than driving itself!

The market today has blended three product categories into one product- the cell phone, camera, hand held video games, and Personal Digital Assistants (PDA's). Have you already forgotten this acronym? The Smartphone market has swept the world. Dozens of companies have left phone carcasses around the world, while new ones enter the market every year.

The obvious example here is the Apple iPhone. Its breakthrough touch screen, smooth interface, and sleek design completely set it apart from other mobile phones. In one swoop, Apple extended its computing skills into a computer that makes calls, and a phone that plays iTunes and takes photos. True, this was a natural extension of the original business. But this was also a quantum leap into a new business with a very large market. Apple has more than 12 percent market share (last I checked). Then, in an equally magic extension, the iPad created a successful computing category that had been pioneered unsuccessfully by Microsoft and IBM a few years earlier.

Product extensions should be done carefully, because they can dilute other products, create tough communications problems with customers, and be seen as meaningless bling with no real product improvement. So far this is not what Apple has done, although without Steve Jobs, predicting Apple's future is difficult. But until recently any way, Apple has exploited its core competencies to create brand new catagories of business so well that they seem to be product extensions.

A close look at Apple reveals warts and product failures as well. Even the best make errors. Look at your competencies as sets of skills. For Apple, they include elegant product design, equally elegant programming solutions, and careful attention to detail. Over the years, starting with the Macintosh computer, it has gained a reputation and customer loyalty few companies enjoy. The Apple brand is one of the world's iconic brands, and it all started in a garage.

Extended Variety

In the 90s, I wrote a column suggesting that the boring computer would need to differentiate itself by color. We had grey and beige then, and for many more years. Recently, I bought a new Dell laptop, my third. What did I buy? Cherry red, of course! Perhaps it was just self-fulfillment, but while we expect the same basic computing quality and features today from laptops, design, color and a few small technical improvements drive our choices. Laptop computer purchases now make a statement about ourselves, as much as what we intend to do with them. People see us in conference rooms, coffee shops, class rooms, and seminars with laptops, notebooks and iPads in a variety of sizes, shapes and colors. Decisions are no longer based on budget compared to the pragmatic processor speed/disk space.

By adding different sizes and colors (and naturally some difference in computing power) to laptops, Dell extended the variety to make sure its customers would not go elsewhere. Dell clearly differentiated its lineup from competitors lacking the depth or foresight to do so, and added a certain "cool" factor to the purchase.

Mobile phones do this with colors (or skins), application downloads, ring tones, and other free or cheap games and services. They use the same phones but add different features to create variety. iPhone joined the fray in 2013 by adding a group of new colors, after touting black, then white in earlier models. Adding colors is what you do when you don't have other differentiators. But this comment is not to detract from the differentiator; Apple had thousands lined up around the world to get it first. They sold millions and ran ahead of production . . . again.

Small, basic industries can be just as transformed as technical ones by differentiation. You may feel this old tactic is a shallow or superficial subject. Yet it is the natural development for most consumer products where a new market is created, grows rapidly, has competition entering the market, and then begins to become a more traditional market. Differentiation becomes personal and psychological, and is an example of the "fashion" phenomena.

In July of 2011, I was on a long flight to Albany, N.Y. My wife sat next to a quiet gentleman. She eventually started a conversation. I was doing research for this book so tried to not get involved, when I heard, "The cookie cutter people from Vermont." Ah, a small businessman. Now I began to listen, albeit with one ear.

Kevin Coleman, controller of Ann Clark Ltd, described how the founder Ann started selling cookie cutters at farmers' markets and festivals in Vermont. Interesting. "How are they doing now?" Molly asked. "Well now we manufacture our own in Rutland, and just bought our largest competitor." Both ears were now engaged with Kevin. We had a short but interesting conversation and exchanged email addresses.

Getting settled into our family "camp" outside of Saratoga, I looked up Ann Clark on the Internet. I was pleased to see a thriving little business, with highly distinctive and engaging recipes and decorating ideas. I realized that two days later we would be passing right through Rutland on our way to my niece's wedding in New Hampshire. I wrote Kevin and asked if we could visit the operation.

I love to visit small factories.

Kevin said he would be happy to host a short tour, so we stopped. What Ann Clark had done was wonderful. An artist, she designed fabulous hang tags for each cookie cutter. These incorporated, through branding, the idea of what every grandmother wants to do—make cookies with her grandchildren. But Ann Clark added creativity. Her illustrations showed how to decorate each cookie and she included her favorite recipes for each kind and shape. This completed the potential for the experience. This was what created the value of each product.

Her success has allowed the business to employ dozens. With the acquisition, this is now the largest cookie cutter company in America. It is in a perfect niche. The market is small enough to keep out big players; the company is big enough to own over a thousand different dies.

Entrepreneurs who recognize how to do something better and open a crack in their marketing are rewarded with profit and success.

Who would think that you could sell one cookie cutter for three times as much as another of the same perceivable quality? Few do, but entrepreneurs who recognize open cracks in a market do, just like Ann did. Just add a little creative, and the price triples!

Increasing the Perceived Quality

Each of these differentiators can influence the four aspects of the Burgess Value Diamond. Perhaps the most desired differentiator is increased quality. Since everyone understands quality/price concepts, wanting to increase quality is understandable. Producers of high end products emphasize quality to justify spending more on their products and go to incredible ends to do so.

Normally, however, the actual quality is a matter of perception. One iconic symbol of this is BMW. For decades they have hammered the quality engineering and ride as the primary differentiator from other luxury-class cars. In the '70s and '80s this notion of "The Ultimate Driving Machine" was all they had to sell, given that BMWs were styled almost as badly as Japanese cars. Today their design is right up there with the best of them.

But from an actual quality measure, they fall behind Lexus and other Japanese cars. Consumer Reports placed them (and Mercedes) way below other manufacturers. Why then, does BMW continue to harp on quality engineering? Because BMW buyers perceive them as having the highest quality and best handling. People who can afford a BMW choose a BMW because of image. BMW buyers either "appreciate" the ride, or believe BMW really does have superior quality. But they also want some way to justify the purchase that is less frivolous than design, or the perception of the best driving machine. This image is slightly different than quality. It's more engineering. If you equate quality with reliability, you're wrong about BMW. That doesn't hurt their sales, however, because buyers are satisfied with the perception of the "ultimate driving machine," whatever that really is.

BMW beautifully makes my point that perceived quality is the goal. I respect all companies that try to improve quality, but many do so and don't communicate it, while others spend extraordinary sums on TQM programs with very small actual increased value. They may have achieved cost savings or reduced product returns. Without the connection with the customer, however, this is a wasted exercise. Every effort should be made to help your customers understand the difference in quality of your product via the Value Diamond, as increased perceived value will yield more sales.

Adding Convenience

Fast food restaurants have changed the meaning of convenience. First we had drive-up restaurants with waitresses on roller skates, then drive-through restaurants. McDonalds is famous for fast service: McDonalds changed the meaning of fast food and set a high bar for competitors that still stands.

While convenience in the restaurant business dramatically transformed the way we eat out, most changes are less earth shaking. Still, the right innovation makes a difference.

Sometimes innovation comes in the form of seeing what another industry has done and adapting it to yours. Starbucks innovated the coffee house in the U.S. by copying cafes in Europe. Auto repair shops added nicer waiting rooms, with coffee, TV and play areas for kids. Here convenience and experience were enhanced. Why take your car to Billy Bob's Tires, with its old dirty waiting rooms, when you can relax and enjoy a clean, comfortable waiting area with Wi-Fi?

Look for convenience in the complete delivery chain from purchase to delivery. Make the purchase easy, clearly lay out all the options and payment methods, provide confirmations and feedback on the purchase or purchase order. Keep customer information for quick access on the next purchase. Let customers know delivery dates and progress on the development of the purchase. Make taking possession easy.

The most impressive business tool since the computer and telephone is the Internet, which can help immensely in providing convenience for many types of customers. All websites should have comprehensive product information, materials distribution and forms for convenience. Increasingly, you need to incorporate purchase data for customer account look-up, auto-fill of data, and access to help desks. Soon you will want to consider rotating products 360 degrees and zooming-in to inspect products online. Fashion sites already have these features. Repeat buyers like the automatic e-order convenience and online tracking now offered by larger pharmacies.

Little things can help to support the "service" quadrant on the Value Diamond, and, as with McDonalds, it can create an entirely new sub industry.

Providing Better Service

Better service can be a result of more convenience. More often, better service is better service personnel or processes. As much of a standard discussion that service is, it still needs constant attention, because people generally deliver it.

Some of my clients use an online advertising service that records conversations between employees and customers. This offers a valuable tool to hear candid conversations and to better assess customer service. I am constantly disappointed by how poorly otherwise intelligent and helpful people can interact with customers on the phone. Conversely, some companies are so good at phone service that the rest of us sound downright rude by comparison.

Start by answering the phone all the time! Sounds easy, but today's phone systems route calls to individuals who have voice mail boxes that only they can answer. But these are *your* customers, not the employee's.

Why would you allow calls to disappear into voice mail black holes? Personal relationships are encouraged, but clear expectations must be set up to insure that all calls are returned promptly, courteously, and with complete accurate information. Central answering by a pro has unfortunately been largely left to technology. I'm convinced that what we save in reception costs is easily squandered with time wasted by constant interruptions from people who are not so "hot" (effective) on the phone. Moreover, constant reminders and training are required to keep phone skills honed. If you want to enhance your service offerings, start by using the phone appropriately.

Don't forget about email services either. If some companies are short on the phone, others are poor with email. Email is a wonderful timesaver in many circumstances. But it can spell disaster for those with poor writing skills, particularly when explaining complex products or providing detailed technical information.

Consider having your best word-smiths write standard paragraphs to be used in most email conversations. Make sure to use the right tone in all writing. Since email erases the emotion heard in the voice, emotions such as concern and care must be written. It's easier to offend in an email than on the phone. Make sure your people understand this.

Fortunately good seminars and websites exist on writing emails. (Google "writing effective emails" and you will come up with several that offer excellent advice.) Ensure your image—indeed, your company—is not tarnished by inferior writing skills.

Standout Packaging

Packaging can tell an entire story about your company. The wine industry, for example, really understands this from an aesthetic perspective. So does Apple. I still remember unpacking my first Macintosh computer. The box was all white (unusual then) with wonderful, full color graphics. When the top was opened, everything was exactly placed in its special place: power cord, mouse (what is that thing?), keyboard. Each was treated as if it were being presented individually.

For the first time in my memory, people in the office stood around, amazed by the packaging and the detail with which each part was presented and packaged. Many now understand that packaging is both functional for damage control and design for image creation. I was impressed at the carefully boxed fan that I bought for just $19. Made in China, the box, packaging and planning for shipment, as well as assembly, was at a very high level.

This care prevents returns, and creates a feeling of quality and organization, even for cheap products. Most foreign companies have not done a good job with the English language, so assembly instructions have been notoriously poor. To meet the demands of buyers, however, they are getting better.

Ann Clark's cookie cutters (discussed above) and Celestial Seasonings (a full story follows in a later chapter) also exemplify how packaging completely differentiates. Celestial Seasonings revolutionized tea and coffee packaging by using local artists and cute drawings of the tea concepts like Sleepy Time, Red Zinger, and Lemon Zinger teas.

Product packaging is an obvious purchase advantage. Great consumer product companies take great care to catch the customers' attention. This is a sophisticated art and science. Smaller companies generally can't afford to compete at this level. Awareness of branding and aesthetics, however, can go a long ways to help design product packaging that will build value. If you need help in this area, seek out industry information and white papers on consumer research for your products.

Customization

Building products to specifications is common in some industries and impossible in others. For industries where customization is rare, figuring out how to give customers exactly what they want is critical to fulfilling their needs.

Customization also provides a certain personalization or buy-in that can create emotional attachments. Perhaps the best example is the video gaming industry. Players can create alter-egos or "avatars" that represent who they will be in the game. One can select a character or body type and then make almost infinite adjustments to create a unique "playing piece." The play itself adds even more customization through what is bought, carried, or used in the game. One of my sons has changed his avatar several times, but his virtual sidekick dog, Hosehead, is always the same. His various groups know his dog and can recognize him by his avatar dog! This has been part of his Warcraft life for over five years now. Talk about how customization can grab customers. This is powerful relationship building stuff.

Customization is not only sticky (causing customers to return), it creates individual and personal experiences, as we saw with ANCO International, mentioned earlier, which used customization to create product differentiation. Re-examine your ability to be flexible in product and service delivery. If this is unusual in your crack in the market, consider this a possible differentiating element.

Faster Turnaround

People love to have their purchasing decisions fulfilled, with the product they bought, as soon as possible. Long lead times to complete the purchase are typically the opposite of what business wants to deliver.

All businesses go through phases where parts inventory, or labor sequence, or special orders slow the process. Seek to shorten and manage these lead times where possible. I challenge you to use Six Sigma, or other continuous improvement process development techniques to shorten lead time before increases in quality. Short lead time is readily understandable to the buyer, while quality increases (except in cases of poor quality) are harder to support and communicate.

All-wood custom window and door maker Paramount Windows, in San Bernardino, CA, regularly works on shortening its manufacturing time. By maintaining high quality and offering very quick turn-around it has managed to survive the worst construction economy in the country. It simply works smarter and faster.

Strong Brand

Creating a strong brand is really the result of the differentiation you create and deliver. All marketers say they understand the concept of brand. I doubt this. Many think it is the promotion used to expose a brand; others think it is a logo. As you might expect, it includes these activities as well as the customer's full experience. A strong brand is one that people recognize and have positive impressions about. They may not know why, but they feel something about it.

Brands are earned the old fashioned way—companies work for them. Positioning your company in your niche also supports or detracts from your brand. When your customers know what you are about, instantly they make decisions and are prejudiced by these notions. Positioning well assists this process by clarifying what you do and how well you can deliver, as well as focusing your company on positioning and brand.

Poor impressions require monumental efforts to correct. Protecting your brand in this sense is critical. Enhancing a brand creates a strong benefit explained somewhat through the PIMS principles. Positioning your company in your crack in the market, with respect to how your brand is perceived, is extremely beneficial.

The reward for a strong brand and leading market share is that you have a larger ability (playing card) to shield your customers from your competitors. The only other very effective similar situation is the relationship.

Aesthetics: "It all starts with the eye." –Aristotle

Each purchasing decision a buyer makes is a multi-sensory experience. Aristotle observed, "It all starts with the eye."[35] Applied to marketing, this means that before we process information about a product, consider the price, or determine the integrity of the salesman, we take in environmental sensory stimuli. The old saying, "You only have one chance to make a first impression," just re-states Aristotle's maxim. Our eyes are the first and most important sense to marketing, but touch, smell, and sound are also important.

Bernd Schmitt and Alex Simonson, in *Marketing Aesthetics: The Strategic Management of Brands, Identity, and Image*, raise the ante on corporate and product image. The notion that corporate image is important is probably not new. However, Schmitt and Simonson show how the aesthetics of product and company are critical to the highest levels of success. If, as a business owner or executive, you have ever entertained doubts about your budget for corporate image, lobby design, product labeling or instruction booklet graphics, this book makes a case even your tight-fisted controller will embrace.

The total aesthetics supporting product positioning is a major differentiator between competing products. Assuming that the quality and service are appropriate for the market positioning, the aesthetics win the sale. "Aesthetics offers multiple, powerful, specific, and tangible benefits to organizations," according to Schmitt and Simonson. The tangible assets of aesthetics include:

- Loyalty: The experience is one of the major "satisfiers" to the buyer.

- Premium Pricing: Due to aesthetics, the perceived value is increased by properly positioned products. Aesthetics cut through information clutter. With thousands of images daily bombarding our lives, only the best are remembered.

- Brand Protection: Aesthetics build bonds with customers that protect against competitive attack.

- Increased employee satisfaction and longevity: Comprehensive aesthetic marketing includes buildings, work spaces, correspondence and transportation. Employees are more efficient, and can be tougher to lure away by competitors.

These are concrete and monetary benefits which cannot be easily explained on a financial statement. Yet hundreds of companies know that the aesthetic benefits are real and carefully craft entire companies around a concept.

Oakley is such a company. Built around innovative design and cutting edge manufacturing technique of sun glasses, Oakley has carved a $230 million chunk out of the high end of the market. A $40 million facility looks like a robot factory out of *Star Wars*, illustrating Oakley's attention to detail and total devotion to aesthetics. The pay-off? Getting $80 for a few bucks worth of glass and plastic.

Absolut Vodka and Ann Clark created new markets by re-thinking the aesthetics. Starbucks did the same by introducing aesthetics into the physical coffee drinking shops. Starbucks has well over a thousand outlets now. What Starbucks created was a place to sit and retreat for a few moments in an environment where total sensory experience brings back customers daily.

But aesthetic marketing is not monopolized by the rich and famous companies. Thousands of very small businesses can and do very nice jobs of coordinating the aesthetic effect of their businesses. They don't generally gain national recognition because they serve small local markets.

Milk is even more of a basic commodity than coffee. Yet, by carefully examining their market and designing a total product, Longmont Dairy has been able to grow and prosper. By developing a market for old-fashioned home delivery, in returnable glass bottles, and combining carefully crafted imagery, Longmont created a new market. With an emphasis on quality, and the cows and plant to back it up, Longmont Dairy can assure customers of the highest standards in taste: so high that Longmont milk lasts as much as 50 percent longer than "store bought" milk. Unlike plastic or paper containers, which can flavor the milk, the glass bottles mean Longmont's taste is unparalleled.

Branding Longmont Dairy Farm milk is an important part of the company strategy. Everything from the logo to the bottles, trucks and invoices has been influenced by the aesthetics developed based on the market positioning. Who would believe that a small company, with limited capital, could flourish by selling milk? It has happened with positioning, aesthetics and hard work.

Marketing "all starts with the eye," but ends with the nose, the ear, touch, emotion, and finally the money. In a market place crowded with products and sophisticated customers, the higher degree of image is the aesthetic one. It's a vital strategic edge in creating perceived value.

Should every company re-emplace their market? A word of caution is warranted. I am not oblivious to the barriers facing a company positioned in the middle of the pack, if it is to move to its own crack in the market. Some barriers are just too large to overcome. Sometimes a company does not have the competencies to make even a small difference in what it does. What typically happens is that the investment is substantial and the ideas are not proven. Risk averse owners are not willing to "bet the farm" on a substantial change.

I recently took on a middle-of-the-pack pest control company, hoping to guide them to differentiate themselves from the large national companies on one hand, and the single person operators on the other. Because the owner was near retirement, radical changes were not really an option. The business challenge here was not only the issue of differentiation, but the issue of competing options. In addition, while the business had been successful for thirty years, the owner's heart was not in the fight any more.

Remember that I started this book by comparing the success of millionaire small business owners with those who just want to make a living. Owners have the option of staying where they are. This is why many small business owners stay small; they are not motivated to become millionaires.

This company had done well in the past, when the owner had large commercial accounts and strong real estate referrals for termite work.

The challenge included a transition from an entrepreneurship to an administratively run business that could work on its own. The problem was not just one of finding a crack; it was a general transition issue as well.

In this industry another barrier is government regulation. Because chemicals and certification issues are the same for all, no real product innovation is possible by a small company. Therefore, the differentiators that remain are image and service. Changing both takes time — years of time. No consultant or branding company can instantly affect either, unless a huge amount of money is spent on media.

Of the other barriers to crack emplacement, many revolve around capital. For example, building factories that can lower production costs enough to kill competition (as Ford did with the production line) is impossible for most small businesses. However, new production ideas born from mental application are available. New distribution networks cost money, as do national advertising campaigns. I could spend a whole book talking about why you can't create a new niche.

Much of *Finding Your Crack in the Market* is about careful observation, analysis, innovation, and patience. Some businesses have very few opportunities to jump into a crack. The question is whether the business owner knows a crack when it opens up, and has the resources and gumption to jump when it feels right.

Small incremental advantages must be taken advantage of when the resources are available to do so. Reviewing your brand when things are tough is a poor time to implement a new long term strategy that is designed to save you. This is a rare hope. Instead, marketing positioning should be a well thought out strategy that attempts to at least capture advantage in the customer's mind. (BMW's "Ultimate Driving Machine" took decades to be really effective.)

Technology, innovation, "Wow" service, and other differentiators, must be carefully used by the small business, based on the right movement on the chess board. Patient execution must happen when the time is right. Small businesses must always assume they will find a new product or better technique around the corner at any time; and be prepared to jump when the opportunity manifests itself.

Chapter 12   Creating A New Market

The more differentiation you can create, the closer you may be to creating a new innovation. It might be said that continual differentiation is a slower type of innovation. The first step in differentiation is finding existing differences in your company/product, compared to your competition, and emplacing your products in the market.   The second step is creating a perceived differentiation in your customers' minds through marketing positioning. The third way is through innovation.

Innovation leads to new products and entirely new categories of products. In fact the single best way to differentiate is to create new products, as already illustrated by several examples. All of those famous companies were small once as well. You can innovate, too. Remember our opening quote from Peter Drucker.

"Companies exist to create customers and innovate.
Everything else is cost."

Smaller companies have an advantage — fewer customers that can be well understood and with whom you have relationships. With your hands on the wheel, you can feel movements in technologies, trends and attitudes among your existing customers. Some of you, like Steve Jobs and Bill Gates, have a sixth sense for what will be cool. The rest of you will have to listen harder to customers. (Bill Gates has long believed in customer surveys, while Apple has sought to maintain a kind of fanatic loyalty. They listen to customers too.)

Many small business people easily innovate, but are less capable at the discipline of creation, budgeting and priority setting required to keep everything else going at the same time. Other authors can assist with this aspect. In *Capturing New Markets*, Stephen Wunker discusses how companies can create new markets. But my role is to point out how innovation can create new cracks in the market. These cracks provide protection and opportunities for the best margins; but other benefits accrue as well.

Wunker, an entrepreneur and corporate venturer, identifies two general ways that new markets can create additional growth other than with existing customers. First, new customers can expand your company. They might create newly affordable or more accessible variations to a new set of customers, similar to yours. But more dramatically, Wunker states, is the opportunity for new consumption: changes in behaviors as a result of innovation.

He uses the examples of Colgate creating a new market with its Wisp toothbrush, an ultra-portable single-use brush. He points to E-Trade, which enabled customers to trade stocks more frequently and economically than with traditional brokers. Each case demonstrates a new level of consumption or behavior that creates a crack in the market that you can fill.

Finding Your Crack In The Market

Many innovations are well known for their success. But the public never hears of many more innovations. These are known only to people close to the crack in the market and their customers. One such innovation is the radio transmitted, internal vibration chip for large industrial motors. This innovation, developed by the University of California at Riverside Electrical Engineering Department and Brithinee Electric, will never be known by those outside the industry. Through software enhancements in programs, Luminex Software, Inc. solved massive and long-standing storage problems for banks by combining software with hardware, tape storage with disk storage.

The vast majority of innovation is also incremental. It builds on existing technology, or style, and adds or re-purposes the elements to create innovation. Few are entirely new ideas. Coffee shops existed before Starbucks, cell phones before iPhones, electric arc lights before the light bulbs, laptops and computer pads before the Kindle and so on. In each case, innovation differentiates the new product from the old. So what the innovation actually creates is a new crack in the market. And the first to occupy that crack gets the resulting business: few others have the innovation or, therefore, occupy the same niche.

Unfortunately, many times it's not the first but the second or third competitor who manages eventually to take most of the market. The spreadsheet VisiCalc was invented by Dan Bricklin. Lotus 123 built a better one. Then Bill Gates, recognizing the concept as a computing staple, built another—Microsoft Excel. The first three phase electrical power generation and transmission system was designed in 1892 for a small California generating plant by an unknown engineer Almerian

Decker; but the industry leaders quickly became Westinghouse and General Electric. The first graphical user interface, the one we all take for granted today on our computers, cell phones, and even ATM's, is credited to Douglas Englebart of NASA in 1962.[36] But it was Xerox that pushed the concept forward by 1973, in association with its copier business. Then Apple introduced it in the first Macintosh computer.

Inventors often are not driven to make money from them and perhaps as a result fail to understand the markets or marketing needs of their inventions. I have met with many inventors who think that the role of marketing is trivial, so their inventions never get launched, or at least, don't get developed as a successful business. But successful small business people, who create a new crack in the market, do understand this. No better examples of modern inventor/marketers exist than Steve Jobs and Bill Gates and the "pitchman" Ron Popeil. But they followed many others like Westinghouse, Carnegie and John D. Rockefeller. John Deere, who saw the need and invented the first cast steel plow that allowed much time to be saved cleaning wet earth from the blade, allowing one farmer to plow many more acres.[37] His 1837 plow development remains as Deere & Company today.

Millions of first innovators are forgotten, but thousands survive in the form of a company, some small and some very large, all having maintained a crack in the market.

Creating Your Own Crack in the Market

One of the most fulfilling aspects of business is the creation of a new product or market. As we have seen, innovation in smaller incremental ways can lead to new markets as well.

Chapter 4 listed the elements that comprise a market: industry, sub-industry, sub-sub industry, geography, further specialization, specification, stickiness and relationship. Each small differentiator allows millions of businesses to occupy millions of small and not so small cracks in the market.

Likewise, every community has a gift shop purveyor that pays close attention to detail, a hole-in-the wall down-home cooking restaurant, a reliable plumber and an honest mechanic (well maybe not every community, but the market always exists for good, honest independent mechanics). These markets develop on the force of their owners' personalities, reputation for quality, distinctive presentation and/or common sense service. As sad as it seems, delivering quality and good service is all it often takes, given really bad competition.

Some business people out-grow their ability to produce and service their customers on their own, so they hire employees. Sometimes the uniqueness does not get transferred to the next employee; the resulting mediocrity leads to decline. To grow the businesses must transcend the simple differentiators of service and quality by adding more sophisticated differentiators through innovation in product development, service, and aesthetics, and perhaps price.

Creating your own crack in the market, by definition, means that you must innovate your product, delivery, service, experience, aesthetics (or other aspects unknown at present) to be uniquely perceived in your market or geography.

Mo Segal – Celestial Seasonings:

In the early seventies, in Boulder, Colorado, I heard about a guy who was picking herbs in the foothills above town and selling natural tea. Later, in a local health food store, I saw the miscellaneous twigs, leaves and herbs being sold in a fashion that I thought was a cover for marijuana. But when Mo Segal starting designing brightly colored boxes with names like Red Zinger, even I, a staunch coffee drinker, occasionally bought and drank tea.

As a 17 year old kid, Mo was dropped off in Denver by his father with $50 bucks in his pocket. Because of his asthma, and poverty, he started hiking in the Rockies looking for and studying herbs as a way to ease his condition naturally. As he developed and shared his tea with fans, he harvested ten large gunny bags. Mo dried his gleanings using old screen doors. The next year he and his friends hand sewed 19,000 smaller bags for more retailers.

"Natural foods" were catching on across the nation in towns like Boulder, as more was learned about the chemicals and growing practices of mega-agriculture. The organic movement grew out of a college-educated population that did not trust big corporations. The baby boomers continued to grow in buying power through the late 70s, and Celestial Seasonings was set to reap the rewards for a completely new crack in the tea market. Lipton, knowing full well what Mo was up to, just laughed off his ideas as "goofy" even as it tried to hire him; Lipton could not understand what had happened.

Such is the fate of the old guard with their eyes closed. Starting with a friend's $800 and a $5000 loan guaranteed by his mother, by 1974 Celestial Seasonings hit one million dollars in sales. By 1979, it had mushroomed to $30 million. Mo believed in herbal tea's healing power and future. He learned quickly how to market to his own generation, and just waited for them to graduate from college and develop a lifetime habit of tea drinking. My wife has maintained a complete inventory of his tea for forty years now. Just as Whole Foods and Longmont Dairy understood this market, Mo cashed in on a very small niche of a niche market. The company eventually sold for the equivalent sum of $336 million dollars in a merger. Lipton was very late in herbal tea business.

Mo Segal had to learn on the job. He started his company with a friend with a business degree; but to build a multimillion dollar company without capital required much more than management skill. It required a ready niche market that was not attacked until he could defend his niche. Mo was creative from the start, and his protected market afforded time and money to grow. If he had come up with a traditional tea product, and bland box, this story would not appear here.[38]

Finding New Markets

In *Capturing New Markets*, Stephen Wunker pushes the methodology forward for intentional market creation. He outlines six categories of issues, or idiosyncrasies, to watch within an industry.

Platform Technology: The astounding rates of new technology developments create instability in old platforms. We have already discussed Blackberry's issues with the "new" iPhone platform. Luminex also illustrates how software adaptations of traditional platforms can create a new platforms.

New Business Systems: Payroll has been around since employees have been around, but payroll systems are now adapting technologies with other software to create full HR management systems. My experience with RMSA illustrates a series of system changes. Using physical cards, RMSA created a service that paired up mainframe computers with smaller retailers to provide high end inventory control. Of course the PC supplanted that system; Cloud-based systems are now developing new systems online that make software delivery a snap. A service bureau supplanted physical paper inventory; software and personal computers replaced the service bureau; and cloud based systems are replacing onsite PC and software systems.

Changing Customer Capabilities: Markets around the world are emerging as the cost of communications drop to levels many emerging economies can now access. Micro-bank loans in India, the ability to bank on a Smartphone, and other innovations are creating access to almost a billion new customers. With technology in the hands of more people new market niches become available.

Changing Customer Behaviors: Everyone looks for these magic points of opportunity, but they are slow to actually happen. Older business people who no longer interact with very young consumers are, unfortunately, even slower to recognize these changes. The Smartphone is a behavior changer that is working its way up the age scale. The continual use of Smartphones to access the Internet, social media and texting communications represents a major behavioral change under the surface, just as the Internet impacted behavior in the mid-nineties. Small business people must watch these behavioral changes carefully to adopt those small things that can create a new market right under their noses.

Changing Business Partner Incentives: Wunker illustrates how an industry ecosystem can change incentives in markets. I tend to discuss this in terms of government actions such as creating economic incentives for renewable energy products. Wunker illustrates how Medicare has changed physicians' incentives to participate in patient IT systems: although systems were available for years, the fact that there was little incentive meant little movement in the market.

Changing Regulations: Obviously, when regulations are instituted, new markets are created. Government has huge potential to change markets. Unfortunately, government rarely makes good business decisions because of political motivations. Still, opportunities are created. The tax accounting and the environmental industry are well known examples. These industries employ people and create business opportunities. (Whether they create general economic prosperity is outside the scope of this book.)

I would be irresponsible if I did not mention the risks of creating an entirely new market. As I have acknowledged, the vast majority fail. It would also be irresponsible not to urge those of you in business, and those of you thinking about business, to maintain the pulse of your customers at all times so you can monitor changes in their behavior or attitude that will erode your crack or open an opportunity for a new crack in the market.

Defending Your Crack In The Market

In *Marketing Warfare*, Ries and Trout suggest that only the number one player in the marketing place should play defense. Everyone else should be on offense.

I can't speak for the big guys. For small businesses, however, it's spot on. As one gains territory each new line should be defended. Often small niches have emerging competitors from unexpected places, so here defense makes a good offense. Sometimes new territory is gained by mistake or a competitor misstep, but if the new line is not part of the strategic objective, it should not be defended; it may be too costly to do so.

A new client in the solar panel installation business is the local leader for solar installations. Through simple referrals, however, he managed to score a cluster of business in a city many miles from home. The strategy is to grow the local market and maintain leadership and brand recognition at home, then move to adjacent communities. But this cluster of business is far from even the adjacent communities. Advertising requires completely different media, his sales people would have to attend different Chambers of Commerce, and travel far for estimates and closes. Meanwhile, the marketing budget would be cut in half for the home front, meaning we might not achieve our objective of increasing his market lead to top-of-mind recall leadership in his town.

This is not much different from the Battle of the Bulge in World War II: the Germans committed so many resources to go on offense that when the advance was completed, they lacked the resources to defend it. They also moved so far (in the bulge) from the front line that they were exposed on three sides; they needed three times as many resources to protect the gain. This worked at the beginning of the war, when no competition was present. (Well the French were there, but ....). By the time of the Battle of the Bulge, the U.S. had invaded Normandy. And for good measure, General Patton was nearby.

This was, of course, foolhardy, a desperate move by Hitler. But it is amazing how small businesses use exactly the same tactics. Another new client wants to open a shop 100 miles from his current headquarters, 50 miles from his "border," when he has a chance to dominate his existing business. Achieving these "Hail Mary" gains is not impossible. But it really taxes resources.

If your current niche is not heavily defended, don't move to another niche.

So how does one defend the current niche?

1. **Always make sure your perceived value is superior to your competition.** Ries and Trout suggest: "Don't be afraid to attack yourself." The constant and incremental improvements on the

elements of value—Service, Quality, Image and Price—keep your competition at bay.

If your competition must compete with your ever-increasing perceived value, they have less money and time to market to your customers and defend their customers. With better and wider customer reconnaissance, you will understand where to put your improvement efforts compared with your competition. Remember to work toward perception, what customers think about your quality, service and price. Don't spend money unnecessarily on sophisticated programs like Six Sigma or Lean, unless you know it will benefit your perceived value with customers.

2. **Block competitive moves into your territory.** This includes competitive increases to their perceived value as well as many other moves they may make. If your competitor drops his price, counter with better quality and service. Make each incremental differentiator a frontal attack on their move. In some cases, you can counter with a price change—but consider the cost in image if prices bounce around.

Legitimate competitor moves should always be matched. The U.S. manufacturers were napping when Toyota introduced the Prius electric automobile. By then, they were too late to block the move. Now they have lots of catching up to do with the electric vehicles.

If your competition introduces new financing innovation, consider your own version to block this temporary advantage.

Meanwhile, keep improving your product and clearly differentiate another decision point.

3. **Play where leaders are expected to play.** You may be the leader in the market, but due to the nature of small business, and obscure little markets, many companies have brands that even the best trivia players could not recognize. (Can you think of the top solar power panel brands?)

   Egos also get in the way. Play where the leaders play. If the leaders are expected to be on the golf course, or on non-profit boards, then pay attention if your customers value these activities. Are the leaders at trade shows, when your ego says you don't need them? Participation in some activities really defines the "players" so be very sure you fully understand this. Each industry is different, so none of these issues are ironclad; but pay attention to customers.

4. **By far the best defense is the relationship.** The genuine trust born through relationships is the best defense you can have for frontal attacks on your business. Meanwhile, never take this for granted. The relationship only protects one or two legitimate competitive attacks. Then you must respond with better value, or lose the trust you have built over the years.

Creating and then defending cracks is, in fact, the usual source of outstanding success.

Chapter 13 Marketing to your Customers in Your Crack in the Market—Positioning and Promotion

Even the top leaders in their respective cracks cannot afford to forget about the competencies that their customers pay them for. Nor can they afford to lag behind changing customer demands or habits. Common mistakes in marketing can open opportunities for competitors. New technology and consumer changes in habits can wipe out entire industries. Companies that invent new market cracks can miss the next rendition of their product. So stay current!

DATA

For all these reasons and more, even market niche leaders must continue to focus on their own customer mix for clues of change. As chapter 9 mentioned, most businesses don't know their customers as well as they should. Sure, attorneys and CPAs think they know everything due to the intimacy of the relationship. But knowing your customers includes: understanding exactly which ones provide the best margins, the most volume, and best, the highest volumes with the highest margins. Most businesses do not calculate the correlation between margin and volume. The large volume customers tend to be the low margin ones. Further, in many businesses, the "care and feeding" of the large guerrilla customers is not even accounted for, creating an even lower margin that is not reflected in costs against that particular customer.

Businesses don't tend to carefully follow changes in the trends among similar cohort groups of customers. By cohort groups, I mean the similarities of customers that group them together in some way. This might be the mix of services they buy, the demographic, or lifestyle (psychographic) similarities. It could be geographic or by industry in the business to business segment.

The vast majority of smaller businesses don't take the time to understand these cohort groups, even though this highly important data is generally contained in some in-house reporting or accounting system. Data contain patterns that can be unlocked.

A perfect example is what Billy Beane and Bill James accomplished with data in the professional baseball business, as nicely illustrated in the movie *Money Ball*. Beane took his Oakland A's to a completely new place by statistically examining who the "value" players were. The data overturned the age-old way of recruiting players and illustrated how, by putting together a statistically balanced team, they could beat teams with superstars. Despite the fact that the team had been stripped of two or three outstanding players, the first season (in 2004) of their new, data derived system, the A's set the incredible 20 game winning streak record.

This kind of earth shattering data exists in all businesses. Monitoring this data and finding patterns, trends and changes is what gives businesses insight about new customers and innovation. In starting their business, owners generally selected a need, trend or pattern in buying. Ironically, many get so mired in their daily operations that they fail on the second most important Drucker principle, to "find customers and *innovate.*"

The pace of change can be dramatic. Old industries is like electric motors evolve slowly (but they still evolve). The fashion business can change six times a year. In rapidly changing and shifting businesses like fashion, looking ahead is in the DNA of good buyers: they simply won't survive if they don't thrive on figuring out what is coming next. High tech is similar: if you don't innovate, others will.

Slower industries, which most are, can be lulled into complacency by their traditional nature. Some industries don't change much, like the buggy whip. But materials change, service levels improve, technology gets applied to manufacturing and office operations. And communication with customers has certainly changed.

Communication

Using internal data about customers and competencies, and external data about competitors provides direction to communications. Data points the way to customer personas and how to "talk to them." Using either the Burgess Value Diamond or SWOT (Strengths, Weaknesses, Opportunities, Threats) analysis can identify advantages and weaknesses in your positioning approach.

In your communications, your advertising, online promotion, sales meetings and materials, use these advantages and your differentiation points in order to <u>clearly illustrate</u> why your product or service is a better match for customers than other less desirable options.

This correlates with finding your target market or prospects, and then fashioning communications to "speak" their language. Some decisions are emotional, so appeal to that as well. Some decisions are more logical, so support logic too.

This sounds easy and obvious. I assure you: very few businesses do this in a concerted way, some not at all. Enlightened business people will see few revelations, they just don't accomplish them!

Brand

My approach, as you may suspect by now, is that a brand is developed using all the considerations above. This must include the aesthetic nature of a brand.

The American Marketing Association (AMA) defines a brand as a "name, term, sign, symbol or design, or a combination of them intended to identify the goods and services of one seller from another." People who specialize in branding will add that it is the emotional and historical reaction that an individual may associate with the brand. History, in this case, will include knowledge and attitudes about previous transactions of the company and competitors. The Coke brand means much to fans, while the hot dog vendor at the baseball game means little to you (unless you have had season tickets for several years).

My take is that a brand must be both the symbol that identifies and the attitude about the symbol. (This can vary among individuals.) It is the sum total of the experience one has had with the brand that *makes* the brand. I am a big believer in the importance of an organization's aesthetic environment (as you remember from Chapter 11) to every brand. When this is good, it is an asset. When it is not so positive, it can be a liability.

Your brand is a key element to communication, so build and protect it just as you would any other asset. Looking deep into customers gives you the opportunity to stay current and innovate when a trend is spotted. Do this through internal data analysis, formal customer feedback, formal complaint resolution systems and watching the general economic trends of each of your customer cohort groups. When you are clearly aware of your brand, and you begin to engage in careful and mindful communication with your target audience, your marketing is ready for evaluation and adjustment.

Branding is not quite marketers' highest calling. It is part of it; but in order and importance branding follows emplacement and positioning. Emplacement includes the market analysis: the size, nature, characteristics and competition; it considers the economics of the niche market. Branding experts usually know that brand development cannot be more important than determining what the market is. The problem is that they typically prefer to leave it to market researchers.

Small business owners must be concerned with their niche market first. How can a brand be developed without knowing this? The classic example is the Nova—the brand mistake of the century. Having developed the brand Chevrolet shipped Novas to Mexico only to realize that the "brand" meant "No VA" or "Doesn't Go" in Spanish. Branding in a vacuum, or putting the brand in front of the market allows mistakes like this.

Ries and Trout say in *Marketing Warfare*: "Only a general with deep intimate knowledge of what happens on the battlefield itself is in a position to develop an effective strategy. Strategy should evolve out of the mud of the marketplace..." In other words, the market comes first. Branding must be the result of the market, positioning and emplacement. My friend and colleague and a Certified Brand Strategist, Russ Cornelius won't disagree with this, although from his perspective, the semantics of branding are slightly different. The point is important, however, because nearly all "marketers" tout themselves as brand experts, and they approach the issue from the creative, not the strategic side. This rarely works in the long term.

Content

Each of these differentiating elements, including your brand, needs to have content built around it. Content is every word, image, video or audio you create to tell your story. The average small business does a poor job creating content. That is, they don't do it at all.

Telling your story, however, is the way of the future (as well as today). Becoming expert in your niche is how you create interest in your solution, product, or idea. As the next chapter elaborates, the Internet is a huge opportunity for most small businesses, if handled correctly. But raw content is required to exploit the power of the Internet. Google is getting so good at finding relevant, authoritative information based on search phrases and personal preferences that expert content is more important than ever. Some search gurus are now saying SEO is dead.

Your new micro-niche is both differentiated and in some ways created by very detailed content that explains why the niche is best filled by your solution. Your customization, fast turn-around, killer service, and superior quality all can define your brand. Each needs the support of content. I'm not talking about a few lines or paragraphs but about the whole story. I'm talking about a dissertation. You simply cannot overdo content on the Internet!

Chapter 14   Finding Your Crack On The Internet

No discussion these days about positioning could be complete without discussing the changes the Internet brings to nearly all businesses.

I was an early adopter of the Internet and co-founded a successful company that has built hundreds of websites and integrated online and traditional marketing for clients. But I can say that while most businesses now have an Internet presence, few are using it properly to promote business. So, this chapter details the changes in all markets that mean you should consider the Internet when positioning and emplacing your company in your crack in the market.

As enormously successful as Amazon has been and as well-known as it is for its huge list of product, Amazon is not commonly noted for what it is actually doing. What Jeff Bezos has really done is to change the 400 year development of the relationship between distribution and the market. First, FedEx changed the time required to deliver products from far away. Then the Internet delivered, to all of us, a communication tool that combined the catalog, telephone, TV, newspaper and store into one easy-to-update medium.

Amazon and other large online retailers have exponentially increased the ability for us to comparison shop, view and select merchandise by using this incredible tool. Amazon is continually pushing closer to the bricks and mortar retailers by decreasing the time and cost to deliver to customers' doors. Amazon will add another dozen distribution warehouses to their existing facilities this year, to push to same day delivery. So Amazon is both differentiating itself from other online retailers, and threatening brick and mortar retailers.

To make the necessary scale of operations work for same day delivery, it has embarked on delivery of food and produce, using its own delivery system. Again, same day! This will not only encroach on traditional retail, but also will threaten grocery stores and smaller delivery businesses such as local organic delivery companies.

More importantly now, Google and others are perfecting search tools that can find multiple inventory vendors, at all locations, for the *same item,* based on UPC code on each package. They have the technology to provide the lowest prices on a specific item. Thus far, they allow only paid search results into the "sort." So, unfortunately, the list will be highly skewed. Bing has started a "Scroogled" campaign to expose this practice. While I hope Google discontinues this practice, it creates an excellent opportunity for Bing to pick up some market share or create a great new market niche for a start-up. One way or another, the trend is simply too huge for Bing or another company not to fill the void, if Google leaves it open.

QR codes and SKU bar codes can now be scanned on smart phones, to bring up that product instantly in a list showing prices. People can view the product in one store and price it in another warehouse or from Amazon. So all reselling of items will need to be completely re-evaluated, and the reselling of items will become hyper-competitive. How will products now be compared? How will they be differentiated? What new cracks are being created? Which old cracks are permanently filling in?

This leads us to the final step in complete disintermediation of product comparison. Disintermediation is the removal of intermediate companies, distributers, and other barriers to products and services. Four hundred years of distribution innovation is now in a completely new era.

Amazon is the distributer and retailer for many products, competing with every other seller on earth for that product. When making products is more profitable than reselling it, Amazon is also making some items. One innovative stuffed animal idea from an individual entrepreneur was copied in China and sold by Amazon. Collectible Supplies, Inc. maker of NFL mascot pillows, noticed a drop in business from 100 to just 20 per day. Amazon had duplicated the product line, and matched his price. They gave featured placement to themselves, so eventually killed Collectible Supplies' online pillow business. [39] And who better to make this evaluation regarding whether to create a knock off copy of your product than the company that sells your product. Amazon has all the stats, so can make informed decisions on proven success that other competitors cannot.

They compete in other ways as well. One Amazon product is the Kindle, which "reads" most of the commercially available e-books, now being uploaded directly by the individual author. My son, Scott, is one of those authors. He sold 30,000 units of his Zombie series in six months. Stephen King (in our family, we now regard King as my son's competitor) did the same with his new book, legitimizing the new publishing paradigm.

Amazon cuts out the publisher, printer, distributer and retailer. The entire book publication process—concept, manufacturing, distribution and selling—can be achieved electronically. It is a parallel universe, one that exists at the same time as the physical one. Of course, the retailers say, "But you can't pick it up and smell it." Okay, a point. But a weak point. Few e-book readers really care. Plus readers can see the cover and several pages online, and can view the author pitching it or the reviews or critics' videos about the product. And most amazingly, with e-book readers, you don't have to wait to get your e-book. No shipper is necessary: even FedEx loses out.

Of course, this isn't the case for every product. Most physical products still require delivery, or even touch; customers want to try it on for fit. So, a few product segments won't be affected. But the book example is well worth thinking about. *This has never happened before.*

Each business needs to rethink each product, name brand and company brand image in a new way, because differentiation based on traditional factors will soon be erased. Companies now must battle for their cracks in the market in both universes.

Brand is Extremely Important on the Internet

The power of search alone can create a crack for strong brands, so brand becomes essential to getting found using "owned" keywords. You will remember the story of Acme Duplex, whose name, like that of Kleenex, defined the category niche. The company had to threaten a lawsuit in order to stop those not selling Acme Duplex from using the term.

Most retailers and distributors have no product brands. They sell other companies' products. They are competitive because of *location* in their crack in the market. They may have higher service levels and expertise that differentiate them, but maintaining a value difference will be tougher as online service likewise increases. Easy access to enormous inventories of goods across the world means the lowest cost seller gets the business (less the cost of shipping from the warehouse closest to you).

Traditional bricks and mortar retailers will rarely be competitive with nationally known brands, unless some kind of status is gained by going to the retailer. Can service and expertise outweigh a 30 percent (or more) difference in price?

In many ways, *your* brand may be the only thing you have left. If Amazon and other huge online stores sell all brands, can you compete with everyone else's brands? Or will you need your own brand that you refuse to sell to Amazon? Will Ralph Lauren website's buyers purchase exactly the same Polo shirt for $95 that Amazon sells for $65?

The mega-online store phenomena is already beginning to change how retail brands are developed and promoted. Companies with strong brands will need to think about losing retail distribution to online stores. Companies with no real control over brands will need to think about developing their own. This takes years, so decisions must be made now, before the reality of revenue drops occur.

Amazon moved to create its own brand and distribution system using the Kindle. Barnes and Noble has long re-published the works of classic authors that are out of copyright, as well as publishing their own local history books using local authors. To meet the competition, they developed their own reading device, the Nook, and they understand that they are locked in a battle with Amazon over content and distribution.

Barnes and Noble clearly understands that to differentiate themselves from their online store and Amazon, they need to create the "experience" of shopping in order to survive. Really, it's all that is left other than carrying the book home. I can spend hours in Barnes and Noble retail stores, which have the ambience of coffee shops. I love the smell of coffee. I love the whole experience as it is! But will I still love it when the hard book inventory is replaced with too many "educational toys." I hope this doesn't happen. Meanwhile, this does not prevent me from buying books from both online competitors.

Because the retail selling of all products is now competing with the experience of online shopping, experience and environment are the biggest differentiators left, unless retailers do a better job at their own branded products that are not online. Fashion will always compete well with the fashion-forward consumer where impulse is very important. But fashion retailers must work hard on creating many new cracks in the market that are not price sensitive and a shopping experience through environment, sound, taste, smell and ambience. People love to go out and shop. It's a social activity. It has been said that shopping is the only "frontier" left to explore as we exercise our hunter/gatherer behaviors. But retailers must ensure shopping continues to feel like a frontier of discovery.

One huge new opportunity for clothing manufacturers is to create options for store branding and design modifications so that store buyers can become design modifiers again, as it was when I was in the retail business. While Wal-Mart and very large retailers do this now, smaller retailers, where the real creativity is, need customization access too. As a retail buyer, almost 40 years ago, I was able to change colors, leathers, lasts (toe shapes), and heels on shoes and boots. They were called "make-up." Don Griffith knew even then that, if we were unique, we could get a couple of dollars more. It was this flexibility that gave me the opportunity to be creative, and together we created lots of very small cracks that produced lots of profit.

Hard goods manufactures will have to provide customization to smaller retailers to accomplish the same effect. Retailers that cannot innovate and "design" their own products will only have convenience and experience left to sell.

On the other hand, what are currently strong brands (Levi, Polo, Nike and many more) will kill their current retail distribution systems if they fail to develop customization. Google can easily find and list products with an identical SKU number or bar code; if the value difference is not perceptible, the low cost provider wins. But if your product is unique, only one will come up. Indeed, Google's search capacity is increasingly sophisticated; at this point, however, search engines are not very good at finding things that are "similar" to a unique SKU. Searching for "similar" in dresses, shoes or sofas will yield an un-usable cacophony of products, and therefore no direct price comparison or competition.

Auto parts are already made to replace part number xyz, so cross referencing can easily be done by Google. Fortunately for auto parts stores, repair is more urgent, and many parts are competitively priced enough to get the business. In-store inventory disadvantages online companies, which can ship quickly but still cannot deliver immediately.

The experience of having "fix it" help in a store remains important. Increasingly, however, online websites have the potential to do the same, or better, with videos and excellent step-by-step help for do-it-yourselfers. Advice and repair videos are extremely popular on Youtube.com. Better, the videos can even be viewed on Smart-phones from under the car!

Competing With the Online Experience

The direct consumer experience, whether it is online, bricks and mortar, or some combination of these, must embrace the experience; because other than convenience, what are the differentiators if not the experience? The key for retailers in physical locations will be creatively rethinking the online experience they provide and integrating it with their on-location experience to refine their crack in the market.

Retailers are starting to use large screen displays in the store to interact with customers. The combinations of Smart phones, computers, internet and video interplay are just beginning to be considered. When these combinations finally take form, it will have as dramatic an impact on retail as Disneyland did to theme parks.

Businesses are scrambling to understand customer engagement through social media. They are collecting email addresses, birthdates, and data on clothing sizes and preferences. They are delivering coupons via email to come into the store. They use Groupon and other pre-purchased discounts and deals. They are tweeting special promotions.

A fashion-forward young women's clothing retailer posts photos of outfits on Pinterest. Having clicked on to the retailer's product page, the customer decides to go into the physical store to try on the item. The slacks she buys need alteration, so the clerk offers to notify her by SMS text message when the clothes are ready for pick up. She gives the retailer her cell phone number. She accepts the clerk's offer to send her an e-receipt. Using the retailer's handy iPad, she gives her email address, effectively opting into their customer email communications. The e-receipt carries cross-sale information related to the outfit she bought in the store. She gives them her birth date so she can get a special birthday coupon. The store now has her history and her preferences in their database. Later, the store curates a new outfit, based on her size and her previous purchase, and emails the suggestion to her. The same email invites her to join their Facebook account for the possibility of winning a free shopping spree. She shares this with her friends. They all start following the retailer.

Currently, the online experience is still dull, albeit very convenient. It makes poor use of full-sized and HD screen capabilities. The closing pitches are poor—nothing like infomercials on TV. Combining interactive graphics and video will enhance the online experience immeasurably compared with today's "billboard" or "brochure" website mentality. Hiking boots will be sold from Patagonia by expert climbers. TV personalities will walk viewers through model 3D homes. Newly developed power tools will be demonstrated on any project you can think of. Industrial solutions will be provided by on-call experts in real time. The nursery expert will discuss every plant variety customized for your climate. Factory equipment will be expertly demonstrated. Cars, airplanes, and motorcycles will be presented through customized simulators, like gaming is today.

As this book goes to press, Audi opened its first digital showroom in the high rent district of Piccadilly Square, London. It closely resembles the vision I just laid out. Huge interactive screens allow "drivers" to open the door, look inside, change colors, rotate and "drive" the cars using touch screens and hand gestures. It's very much like Microsoft's Kinect, with controller-free X-box gaming. Kinect responds to your voice as well as to how you move.

Thousands were sucked inside to see Audi's car-less showroom. Did it work? Yes. Audi increased sales 70% and the margins increased 30% on the sale! The total immersive engagement of the experience sold the cars. In the high density of a city, selling without cars works.

Nor is this the only early success story.

Razorfish, the digital marketing, branding, and advertising agency that designed the Audi showroom, also designed a high-tech store in Chicago for AT&T. What could you possibly do for a telephone company when everyone knows what it does? Focusing on interactions, not transactions, Razorfish sold a story: "What cool experiences AT&T brings to your devices." With 150 displays around the store, and a 20 foot mega wall, the experience broke down barriers between the phone sales people and customers. This brought 30,000 people per month through the doors! Accessory sales increased 300 percent.

As you can see, the possibilities are infinite—only restricted by your company's innovative juices. In some ways, the Internet will be vastly superior to the physical store, or company sales presentation. In a retail store, the presentation is only as good as the hired help. Rarely can someone be professional all day long. And employees cost a lot. In order to compete, the retail environment must be supplemented by in-store display and pitches from the pros.

Not all experiences will be supplanted with the video display. I doubt that Disneyland will ever replace its physical experience—which, of course, has for many years been augmented by images and videos. The difference is that now this technology can be built and delivered anywhere for much less than the cost of Disney's development teams.

The Haunted Mansion's live-looking talking heads and skulls now hang from the porches of private homes on Halloween.

Already in the early nineties I wrote an article about the "Disney-fication of Retail." My thesis was that millions of people have witnessed for themselves world class standards. McDonald's set the standards for speed (one they have lost today). As a result, every American understood what fast-food meant at its best. Likewise, millions of Americans have experienced a Disney park, where the standards were set for the park experience itself.

I emphasized that service and experience should increase at the retail store as competition heated up. In fact many retailers did get it. Barnes & Noble, as mentioned earlier, gets good marks for the experience created with their in-store coffee shops, an idea independent book stores brought to fruition years before. Starbucks is famous for selling the experience along with its "special" coffee, the concept being borrowed from the European café. Bass Pro Shops probably comes closest to my vision for a retail niche, bringing a rustic outdoor experience indoors, showcasing merchandise including their own brand, and expertly demonstrating the merchandise that consumers want to understand, sold usually for a reasonable or lower cost. Bass has established new standards for the retail experience, strongly defining their market niche. Unfortunately the Bass website is an uninspiring electronic catalog in which all of the store experience has been squeezed out. This is short sighted: they need to blend both together.

Finding Your Crack In The Market

All the thousands of micro niches that existed for consumer products will be readjusted over the next several years as the distribution models are forever changed, just as the train overtook the canal boats and the catalog created shopping by mail. There is a slow motion earthquake in these millions of cracks in the market. Some cracks will be completely destroyed even as new cracks are created; others will erode into valleys only the big boys can capture.

The concept of product and company positioning for success is still exactly the same. Find your own crack in the market, one that you can dominate with little competition. Your decisions about how to position your company during this slow but inexorable earthquake will shape the profitable products you offer and the brands you create.

Your job is not to "update your website." It is to study the entire Internet and its possibilities to feel your way through the competitive landscape: to evaluate what online sales closing means to your business; to understand the benefits and pitfalls of social media; to examine the backend programming possible to provide customer services online; to maximize the effectiveness of PR in this new environment; and to showcase your company's competencies and expertise in a way that convinces customers (and Google) that you are indeed an expert.

These are the bigger issues for your company to examine, without getting bogged down in the technologies of doing all the work online. If you can, outsource as much as possible with experts you can learn from. The Internet will change the way business is done and shift small niches.

Grabbing Your Online Niche

Smaller businesses spend most of their time making each day work: talking to customers, fixing problems, listening to vendor pitches. Most business advisors agree that you must make time to work ON the business instead of spending all your time working IN the business, day to day. Good advice.

Working ON their Internet presence is one area very few businesses properly assess. I can't emphasize this enough. **Marketing promotional activities have changed more in the last ten years than the previous 150 years.** And most good, leading companies don't even know it.

Sure, these days every business has a website. But that is like saying you have an office. The question is can anyone find it? Getting found by search engines is similar to your physical niche. You must be on the first page. The top three is preferable. Taking all the spots is ideal.

The Internet is even more important than a few years ago because of new technology for accessing the Internet. People will see your website from their phones, iPods, laptops, computers and touch screens around the world. Your customers will be looking up your parts from the field on their cell phone. They will want to reference your expertise from the library on their iPad, and will want to interface their company's PO system with yours from their desktop at work. Since their experience will vary from one device to another, you need to plan your website pitch for each one to maximize its effectiveness.

This client must occupy the online niche as well as the physical niche. Their online crack in the market must be located by Google and Bing. This market is defined by the search terms that customers use to find services needed, in this case, electric motor repair. This can be qualified by adding the business city. If they come up first world-wide, at least with respect to those search terms, they will be exposed to everyone using those search terms.

Defining Your Online Niche — Keywords

Search terms or keywords become the micro-niche online. If you sell "big pumpkins for jack-o-lanterns in Omaha," you had better get found when your prospective customers search on "pumpkins Omaha." If not, you simply do not exist for that customer. If you are in the top three, great; if on the first page, good. If not on the first page, it's really bad. Your chance of a visit drops to less than five percent on the second page.

Getting found when someone is looking for what you offer is the key issue and determinant of your success. If you want the Internet and smart phone search business, you will need to focus on the Internet search niche, including by considering those hundreds of thousands of phrases that people search with. Keywords represent a business's niche market.

Broad single words generally represent larger markets. Search modifiers- such as location, specialty, or purpose—represent smaller and more specific markets. Again, being first, second or third in the search offers the same leadership position as in the market. In the future, more and more businesses will in fact create leadership ON the Internet before they do in the market. At least for some industries, search will create market leadership.

Specializing in smaller and smaller niches is very easy on the Internet. In fact this is necessary when you start your battle. Large markets can cost millions of dollars to capture. Getting the "insurance" market is very expensive. Developing the "property and casualty insurance in Rockford" niche is easier. And if you specialize in "bass fishing boat liability insurance in north Rockford," and you post in-depth expert content on this subject on your website, your niche has an excellent shot at being found . Small businesses can be more successful because they find small niches to occupy and dominate rather than trying to be everything to everyone. That specialty must continue online.

Caution here for those of you who never advertise, given your reliance on referrals. Today, even referrals look online to validate businesses. If you look different (or worse) than the image portrayed by your referrer or if buyers can't find your website, you will turn off many younger buyers, even with a referral.

Market Emplacement Online

The battle over keywords is already over for many who arrived late to the website party. Sure, anyone can buy Google Ad-Words if a website's natural search is poor. But this can get very expensive. "Owning" key phrases (continually coming up in the top three) is like owning that market, allowing your website high ranks in search engines on those phrases. Some search words have high barriers of entry, such as "bank" or "insurance." They must be modified into phrases like "banks in Baltimore" to get a fighting chance. Even then, small banks will not be able to add web pages fast enough to dislodge the big banks whose carefully built websites own those keyword terms. Additional terms like "community" might be added, but to little effect.

Nondescript industries are also a challenge online. The huge word "fulfillment" describes not only an activity but also an outsourcing industry. This industry has some specific words to describe parts of the process venders would use to search with, such as "Pick and Pack." But overall, general descriptions are used for services to fulfillment of the manufacturing or inventory picking process. For example, if you search "System Integrators" you are unlikely to get useful results. So targeting obscure terms as market differentiators also has a high cost of entry.

Instead, services and slogans must be developed to emplace the bank online using new phrases that are not currently used. "Executive Privilege Banking in Baltimore" might get some kind of search result, but this would need to be supported by strong advertising so people would use it almost as a brand. I would trademark any phrase I am going to use as an online differentiator. Brands that are unique can be part of market emplacement online. Naturally, they should tie to a real market.

You do own your name. So use it effectively. People generally look for information by typing descriptive phrases, company names and brands, or questions. So, the fact that your company name is used indicates that your brand is already known. This is great: you have a decent chance of being found.

Type Coca Cola. Coca Cola website pages fill the search page. Most are authorized company or distributer websites, some are news about the company or product, and a few are social media sites owned by Coca Cola. Because the company will legally protect its brand, the non-official websites that show up are merely targets for the lawyers.

Google tries to provide the best search resources and works hard to provide Coca Cola pages, not imposters' pages. Typing in "cola" will turn up all kinds of colas, representing the drink (from several companies), acronyms representing organizations, concepts or processes, and other miscellaneous websites.

The meaning of the search term changed and so have the results. This is the problem when working with search engine optimization. In terms of carbonated beverages, Coca Cola owns the cyber space niche as well as the physical one.

But consider "Paramount." We see movie studios, definitions, and movie review sites. I have three clients with Paramount in the name. One is Paramount Windows and Doors. If the search is modified (adding windows and doors), no less than three companies with the same name turn up. Fortunately, only one is in Southern California. One is in Canada and one in Arizona. But users must hope that the right one comes up, or they might just buy from the wrong one!

Then try "windows and doors." Where I live, Paramount Windows and Doors is high because of Google's local search preference. But most of you will see Anderson and Pella windows among your local results.

Customers and distributers will use the full Paramount Windows and Doors key phrase, but prospects and shoppers won't. They will use the descriptive phrases. You see the problems? First, common words used in names are difficult to capture in search. Second, the full name must be used in these cases for any hope of being found, and this only works if the user knows the name. Third, descriptive terms have much more competition.

Our goal for Paramount Windows and Doors is to get found under all combinations of "windows southern California," "doors southern California," and all the cities in the area as well (hundreds of them). To the extent we succeed, we can hope to receive that proportional amount of the search traffic.

We knew this would be a problem, so we started with key phrases we could win on, such as "custom wood windows southern California." This is a phrase that we can become expert in, online, because it is a small niche, and the company is, in fact, expert on the issue. Paramount focuses precisely on this business and doesn't need to be listed with plastic clad or aluminum windows. The customers who want the real thing, and are willing to pay for it, know to add "wood" to the search. The content written at this very small niche level is an important part of why the page is top in a Google search. Other factors are relevant. But this case illustrates how small the niches should be online. Yes, hardware, glass, and types of windows are further refinements. Joint types and methodologies of construction are even smaller refinements. Each represents a very small market crack. Each must be fought for online.

"Owning" brands and slogans that can be trademarked gives you control over powerful keywords, allowing you to compete successfully as you develop the best content on your website. Every feature, slogan, product name and brand we develop with clients gets a full search evaluation before we present it to the client. Branding is crucial in differentiating your company; the value will be higher for brands that are well thought of. The words and phrases used for brands cannot be well evaluated without considering the online component.

Finding out how often a keyword is used is a way to determine the size of the online market. You can get detailed search counts and competitive key word strength. If your own webmaster cannot do this, find one, or a marketing consultant, who can. Currently, most small webmasters cannot afford these tools, so larger specialists in website search are sometimes necessary to analyze how well your website is positioned. In any case, it is the cheapest marketing research you can do. This data shows how many people search on, for example, "double hung window balance" versus "Acme Twin." The generic results for the description are many times more than the "brand" keywords. Programs can also determine how many indexed pages your competitors have and what keywords are recognized. You can find out exactly how many times a phrase is used online each month. These are very useful in understanding the budget you need to develop in order to maintain your edge online.

Remember, if your website is not easily found, you will only have a physical market. Moreover, that physical market will undoubtedly shrink as the Internet continues to expand. However, if users search on your brand or product name (unless you sell to Amazon!), you have the best chance of getting the web traffic. The effort is worthwhile in real dollars and cents.

Keeping your website effective is a continuous job, just like advertising. It will not go away. Adding pages that describe your particular products and differentiations must be an ongoing project or your competition will catch up.

Cyberspace is a parallel business universe to the physical one we live in. It is already important and will be more so in the near future. If you don't take leadership in the search niches you are in, you will be at a distinct disadvantage. The good news is that just a very few companies really "get" what is happening, so the door is still open for many industries. But, don't wait.

Chapter 15 Summary

This book identifies the major factors that contribute to exceptional success for small businesses. By exceptional success, I mean a business that employs people, contributes to the community, and creates wealth for its owners.

Probably some additional factors contribute in specific circumstances, but every successful small business has, in large part, the characteristics discussed in this book. Business success factors include:

A previously un-recognized product/ (service) and/or differentiator, or simple luck

Dominant position in its crack in the market

The delivery of greater value to customers

Entrepreneurial family (or the right personality)

Of course, other characteristics also matter. But I have not seen extraordinary success last without these four. If you are thinking that you succeeded without these four pre-requisites, you may be an incredible and lucky business person — or perhaps you just have not failed yet.

Many business people might have been included in the list of the successful, if only they had recognized when to sell and retire.

If you really do not have a crack in the market, are not in the top three in market share, then I suggest you either get out while you can, or fight to stay in the top three. Because eventually your niche will consolidate. It is the natural order of markets. If you continue in the middle of the market, your margins will eventually drop, creating a mediocre return on investment.

Meanwhile, many sharp (but unsophisticated) business people do well in terms of profit. But upon further investigation, when real ROI over many years is calculated, their returns are much lower than in their industry or from other investments. With extreme conservatism they accumulate some money. Still, it's a poor use of the money.

One illustration of this situation was a hardware store that was for sale. After a lifetime of work, the owner decided to sell. But no one would agree to his price. Over thirty years, he had accumulated inventory that his accountant continued to value at cost. (Since the cost of a hammer always goes up, the logic was that all hardware owned should go up.) Because he rarely cleared inventory, it accumulated on the books and in the basement. What was reported as profit on the income statement simply flowed through to the balance sheet. Because the inventory was never properly valued, no write downs were made, meaning that the profit was never properly adjusted down for the losses. The market price of the business was millions of dollars lower than the book inventory that the CPA had allowed to exist on the books, let alone any "blue sky" value. While the owner had accumulated some other assets than the business, the realization that he was millions of dollars poorer than he thought was a hard lesson to learn near the end of his life. Unfortunately, this is common. If you think your business is part of your wealth, consider this example carefully.

Many businesses don't properly calculate profit against investment, so they simply think they are better off than they are. PIMS would support the notion that, in reality, this type of business substantially under performs against its competition. But this reality is simply hidden due to lack of understanding. If your business is like this one, have your CPA read this example and then re-evaluate your profit and ROI performance.

Of course, this is your crack in the market. Getting started in business can happen simply through fortitude. Great sales people can do this. They can make some money, but not really create a business—it won't survive past the sales shtick. But to prosper, the going is much easier if you have a different approach or a new idea. Even then, most don't make it. But when they do, growth can happen faster and with higher margins. The PIMS principles powerfully demonstrate this, and I have observed and demonstrated this over the years with my own clients.

Dominant position in its crack in the market

The PIMS principles demonstrate that when customers believe quality is better and the company has leadership in the market, customers will "reward" you with higher margins. This is about as axiomatic as business can get. The PIMS database is composed of larger businesses, but again, this is also true in small business. Jack Trout and Al Ries, in "The 22

Immutable Laws of Marketing," cite market leadership as the first law.[40] "It's better to be first than to be best," they say. This is because the companies that create brands or niches first are the ones most likely to be remembered. Ries and Trout cite a relationship of market share where the first is twice as big as the second, and the second is twice as big as the third. So a leader in the niche with a 40 percent market share has a competitor (number 2) with 20 percent. A third competitor has 10 percent of the market. This leaves 30 percent for all the rest to fight over. People like to buy the leading product. Certainly in Business to Business (B2B), no one ever gets fired for buying from the leader.

If you are not a leader in the market, find or create a crack where you are. Using somewhat different language, Ries and Trout say, "Create a category you can lead in." They cite the example of the person who was first to fly the Atlantic Ocean. Everyone knows Charles Lindbergh did this. He wasn't the best aviator, but he was first. Barely anyone remembers the second one. How about first woman to cross? Amelia Earhart. She created a new category— first woman. Indeed, no one remembers her for another fact about her flight, that she was the third person.[41]

Both points support my premise that finding your crack in the market is essential.

Delivering greater value to customers

If you have your own crack and you are the market leader, the best way to maintain that market position is to continually deliver greater value to your customers. Overall value includes "better" quality, service, price and image. I have said that if you have what people want, they will beat a path to your door to get it. Like spontaneous combustion, others tend to notice all those people rushing to your door, and soon others will beat your value, or replace your innovations with an acceptable alternative. The only way to keep your business is to continue to be at least somewhat competitive with value.

Entrepreneurial family (or the right personality)

In the U.S., people of all walks and backgrounds are millionaires. A few characteristics are common among very successful business people. If you don't already have these, you are not precluded; but having these characteristics is common to them:

Financially conservative

Supportive spouse

Intelligent *enough*

Natural understanding of people

In chapter 7, I outlined research on millionaires, showing that the above characteristics are among the key ones. Business owners (or their spouses) who spend the money they make as they become successful will not have enough money to grow the business. By necessity successful business owners must be conservative. Spouses who are supportive in other ways (emotionally, mentally, by taking primary care of the children and perhaps even working in the business) contribute to the likelihood of success.

When those first people are hired, treating them appropriately is crucial to getting others to do what you used to do. Tyrants and impersonal owners can succeed, but it's tougher. Small business millionaires share this ability. You can acquire this talent if it does not come naturally to you, but you must understand your shortcomings in order to do so.

Once these four key characteristics are in place, business owners must use all their smarts to learn the key tools necessary to keep the books, motivate people, watch competitors, and keep track of customers. Some do this intuitively; most do not. The people who really do make it and create wealth are not all expert leaders, wonderful entrepreneurs, geniuses, technical wizards or MBA's. This is because good business management practices can be learned by those who are smart enough. You need enough smarts. Having much more than that however, helps little.

Being tenacious is more important than being really smart. Understanding people goes a long way toward success compared with being very smart. The virtues of hard work, honesty, ethics, and care for the customer all trump academic ability. These American values and the individual freedoms we still have in small business are why most of us can succeed even without a formal business education. The small business person is the surviving individualist of pre-revolutionary era freedom.

Post Script

The story of small business success is the story of American success. Small businesses have historically invented the majority of new innovative products and services. We are the first to hire when recovering from a recession, and we continue to hire.

Few businesses start big, the railroads and a few stock companies being the rare exceptions. Rather, businesses grow big over time, as their small crack in the market expands to a larger one, and they maintain their leadership in those markets. As the crack turns into a valley, many more small cracks, tributaries to the valley, emerge allowing seemingly similar companies to exist in similar industries, but slightly different niches.

The companies that do well and thrive are leaders in each market. The others languish with lower return on investment, remaining also-ran companies, or eventually wither and die. It is difficult. The vast majority of small businesses never celebrate their three year anniversary. Just a few see five. Unsuccessful owners generally lose their life savings, family money, sometimes their homes, and usually their pride. It's an amazingly harsh sentence, yet follows the natural order of things perfectly—survival of the fittest.

This system over the years has created the highest standard of living the world has ever known for the masses of workers. The owners, the small percentage of survivors, can profit greatly while contributing to customers, community and employees.

Understanding who and why these business owners do succeed has been a topic over a century of investigation, creating business schools, management texts, marketing education, the accounting profession, and countless additional self-help programs on how to succeed. It has become an industry itself. The simple point is that if people do something new, albeit simple, they can prosper in spite of themselves.

They successfully fill a crack in the market.

Yes, they do need a certain level of intelligence. They need to get along with and at least marginally lead people. They are ethical, work very hard and smart, and they maintain time for family life and friends. They are confident and have great integrity. They are fiscally conservative.

But most importantly, they:

1. *fell into a crack in the market and worked diligently to serve customers, or*
2. *had the vision to see an opportunity in an underserved market and worked diligently to serve customers.*

When either of these two critical pieces comes about, and a company fills it well enough to be one of the top three leaders in the market, customers reward the company with higher prices, margins, return on investment and the coveted leadership they want to participate in.

Here lies the barebones of small business success.

This is not to minimize any of the additional work and cunning that goes into a business skill and the competency necessary for each business niche, the production process or attention to detail in the market. It is simply to say that, for whatever reason, if the owners possess the basic elements so that their company consistently fills a niche market, it has a real chance to succeed and create wealth. Dominating a small niche provides profits that can be reinvested.

Sometimes it even takes practice. Lots of millionaire businessmen failed a time or two before they learned the basic skills necessary to run a business. Many may have learned that they had no crack in the market to start with, but *found one the next time around.*

On the other hand, hundreds of thousands of those who *should have succeeded* didn't: business graduates, attorneys, public accountants, business professors, and former Fortune 500 executives.

Trained formally or by experience, business people must find a crack in the market and serve their customers better in some way. Some recognize their gifts, some do not; all had some lucky circumstance come their way.

Having the training is optional. Finding a crack in the market is not.

1. Highly successful small businesses (measured by wealth creation) usually **occupy a leading position** in a very narrow market niche. Some companies just fall into a crack in the market by chance, and others work to specifically develop solutions for a problem in a very narrow niche.

2. A small percentage of niches and new cracks in the market actually **innovate new products or services** that create entirely new niches in the market. Innovation serves to differentiate and even create market niches.

3. **Purchasing decisions are driven by perceived value**. Small companies continue to exist when there are incremental increases to perceived quality, service, pricing options and image.

4. **Acquired leadership in the market creates success.** The PIMS principles, marketing data, and top marketing consultants confirm the thesis that leadership is the number one immutable Law of Marketing. Winning market share in a small niche is the major strategy for wealth creation.

5. **Management prowess is secondary to leadership in a niche market.** The overriding issue is whether people want the product. If they do, the company will be rewarded with **higher margins**. There is little direct relationship between management competency and success in small business in small niches. While management competency is always a plus, it is unnecessary in tight niches.

6. **Market Intensity drives the requirement for sophisticated marketing.** If the market is not crowded and demand is high, margin and success can follow. Better marketing strategy is the only solution in the face of heavy competition.

7. When little market intensity exists, and demand is not met by the industry leaders, **a vacuum is created; this will draw competitors into the niche**, unless high barriers to entry are present.

8. The process of moving or creating a leadership position in a niche market is called **marketing emplacement** and includes **marketing positioning**. Tools that enable businesses to evaluate their competitive edge include understanding the nature of markets, perceived value, differentiation and brand evaluation.

9. **Emplacement should occur in both the physical world and cyberspace.**

Building Blocks of

Small Business Wealth Success

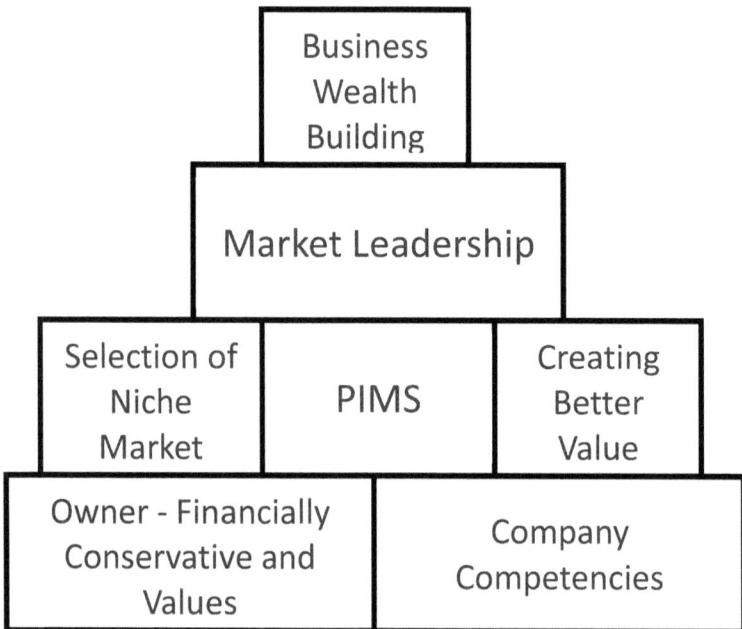

INDEX

END NOTES

[1] William A. Meyers (1983), <u>Iron Men and Copper Wires</u>, Interurban Press, p. 11.

[2] Many history sources place this in other communities, but the Henricus re-enactors believe otherwise. Henricus Historical, Ferrar's Island, VA.

[3] Clifford Dowdey (1966), <u>The Virginia Dynasties</u>, Crown Publishers, p. 99.

[4] Dowdey, pp. 147-172.

[5] Meyers, p. 11.

[6] Jill Jonnes (2004), <u>Empires of Light, Edison, Tesla, Westinghouse, and the Race to Electrify the World</u>, Random House. pp. 87-1-7.

[7] Jonnes, pp. 241-246. General Electric also purchased Hot Point who made electric irons, and many more small companies.

[8] Bottled Water Boycotts: Back-to-the-Tap Movement Gains Momentum

, Janet Larsen, http://www.earth-

policy.org/plan_b_updates/2007/update68?gclid=CNT6mYf0jLsCFeZ7

QgodQAsA-Q,

"The U.S. Conference of Mayors, which represents some 1,100 American cities, discussed at its June 2007 meeting the irony of purchasing bottled water for city employees and for city functions while at the same time touting the quality of municipal water. The group passed a resolution sponsored by Mayors Gavin Newsom of San Francisco, Rocky Anderson of Salt Lake City, and R. T. Rybak of Minneapolis that called for the examination of bottled water's environmental impact. The resolution noted that with $43 billion a year going to provide clean drinking water in cities across the country, "the United States' municipal water systems are among the finest in the world."

[9] The Three Big Ideas, film on three best-selling business books. http://www.the3bigideas.com/

[10] Malcolm Gladwell (2009), <u>What the Dog Saw, and Other Adventures</u>, Back Bay Books, pp. 3-35.

[11] What the Dog Saw, Malcolm Gladwell, pp 30-31.

[12] Robert Buzzell and Bradley Gale (1987), <u>The PIMS Principles</u>, The Free Press. The PIMS database, managed by the Strategic Planning

Institute, now offers reports using the data of outside companies. This single landmark book outlines the "secrets of marketing" that every business should know, but a minuscule number do.

[13] Buzzell and Gale, p. 195

[14] Jonathan Burton (Aug 2, 2012), "Follow the Buffet Strategy; Investors try to cut risk with funds that look for entrenched businesses," *Wall Street Journal*. See also http://wiki.fool.com/Moat.

[15] Competitive Strategy (Free Market Press, 1980) is one of Michael Porter's earlier works on techniques for analyzing industries and competitors. This on and his later books are excellent sources for business executives in very tough markets who need a more detailed analysis.

[16] Charles G. Koch (2007), The Science of Success, John Wiley & Sons.

[17] Koch, p. 107. Porter concurs with the PIMS data regarding "Stuck in the Middle. He says that "a firm failing to develop its strategy in at least one of the three [diffentiators] –a firm that is stuck in the middle—is an extremely poor strategic situation" (pp. 41-42).

[18] Koch, p. 55-57.

[19] Koch, p 60-61.

[20] Thomas J. Stanley and William D. Danko (1996), The Millionaire Next Door, Longstreet Press.

[21] Stanley and Danko, p. 8.

[22] Stanley and Danko, p. 6.

[23] Kaufman Index of Entrepreneurial Activity 1996-2011, p. 6 chart. Kauffman Foundation of Entrepreneurship. Women form businesses at the rate of approximately .22 percent of the population, while men do so at .43 percent of the population, making women responsible for about 1/3 of business formation.

[24] Kaufman Index of Entrepreneurial Activity 1996-2011, p. 9 Figure 4.

[25] Thomas J. Stanley (2000), The Millionaire Mind, Andrews McMeel Publishing, p. 13, Table 1-1.

[26] Harvard Professor David McClelland challenged IW tests way back in 1973 as a predictor of success. His work suggests that academics find difficulty in demonstrating that grades in school are related to other behaviors of importance—other than doing well on aptitude tests (cited in Stanley, The Millionaire Mind, p. 68).

[27] Malcolm Gladwell (2009), Outliers, The Story of Success, Back Bay Books, p. 80.

[28] Stanley and Danko, 1996, p. 12.

[29] The full quote is "Because the purpose of business is to create a customer, the business enterprise has two–and only two–basic functions: marketing and innovation. Marketing and innovation produce results; all the rest are costs. Marketing is the distinguishing, unique function of the business." http://www.forbes.com/2006/06/30/jack-trout-on-marketing-cx_jt_0703drucker.html

[30] Al Ries and Jack Trout (2001), Positioning: The Battle for Your Mind, McGraw-Hill p. 19.
[31] http://ries.typepad.com/ries_blog/positioning_debate/
[32] Al Ries (1996), Focus: The Future of Your Company Depends on It, Harper Collins, pp. 109-113.
[33] I say "every" in the general sense. Government regulation regularly changes the demand and/or supply of markets. By spending money on pet projects or increasing regulatory power, niche markets are altered, destroyed, and created.
[34] Bernd Schmitt and Alex Simonson (1997), Marketing Aesthetics: The Strategic Management of Brands, Identity, and Image, The Free Press, p. 102. Information from interviews with the owner, Sam Farber.
[35] Schmitt and Simonson, p. 85
[36] Jeremy Reimer (2005), A History Of the GUI, http://arstechnica.com/old/content/2005/05/gui.ars/
[37] Jeffrey Waldron (nd), "Mr. Deere's Self Scouring Wonder," The Fortnightly Club of Redlands. http://www.redlandsfortnightly.org/papers/waldron.htm; and http://brenda-inventions.blogspot.com/2008/08/who-invented-plow.html
[38] From Executive Insights, Leeds School of Business, University of Colorado interview with Mo Segal, 2008. Some information from the Celestial Seasonings website.
[38] Al Ries and Jack Trout (1986), Marketing Warfare, McGraw Hill, p. 188.
[39] Wade Forest of Razorfish, at the San Diego Interactive Day, June 19, 2013.

[40] Al Ries and Jack Trout (1994), <u>The 22 Immutable Laws of Marketing</u>, HarperBusiness, Kindle Version, Chapter 1.

[41] Ries and Trout (1994), Chapter 2.

[42] The Wall Street Journal Online,
http://online.wsj.com/news/articles/SB1000142405270230444140457748 2902055882264

[43] The 22 Immutable Laws of Marketing" Perfect Bound, Kindle Version, Chapter 1.
[44] Ibid., Chapter 2

[45] The Wall Street Journal Online,
http://online.wsj.com/news/articles/SB1000142405270230444140457748 2902055882264
[46] The 22 Immutable Laws of Marketing" Perfect Bound, Kindle Version, Chapter 1.
[47] Ibid., Chapter 2

Bibliography

Many books have influenced my thinking over the years since business school. During my years in the field in the mid-west as a retail-merchandising consultant, I read motivational books to increase my knowledge of sales. On long days between towns, I listened to tapes by the great Zig Ziegler (father of sale training, in my view) and Brian Tracey. I will never forget a statement Tracey made concerning knowing your subject: "Most people stop learning when they leave school. So if you just read one book a month on a subject, in just two years you will have read 24 books, making you an expert; in five years, 60 books making you as well versed as most Ph.D.s." I took this principle to heart.

I generally read from 12 to 15 non-fiction books per year. I use a pen to underline every important concept for quick review. The books are divided about equally between business (heavy on marketing, of course), and history (heavy on business history) with about a 10 percent mix of science and political science. The best books I have read or reviewed several times.

For many years I have also subscribed to Soundview Executive Book Summaries®, which reviews the best-selling business books and condenses three or four a month; some of these make it into my reading list.

Below are the books that I consider the real ground breakers. These influenced my practice and thinking on the principles articulated in this book.

They are intentionally ordered in a way to help business people develop an education in how small business works. Titles that are quick reads are indicated by an asterisk (*) in front of the title.

Think and Grow Rich, Napoleon Hill, 1937, published originally by the Ralston Society. The book has had many re-prints, and been republished by many others.

> This is the granddaddy of all motivational books. It was effectively "commissioned" by the great industrialist Andrew Carnegie, who challenged Hill to study great wealth builders and discover the secrets of their success. The book was founded on Hill's earlier work *The Law of Success*, which reported on twenty years of Hill's research in individuals who achieved great wealth. *Think and Grow Rich* condensed the laws of success and offers a philosophy of personal achievement. It recalls a time in America when references to God and faith did not embarrass society. Do not discount Hill's insistence on bringing religion into the discussion. In fact, it could be refreshing, given our current moral issues in government, politics and business.

Small Is Beautiful, Economics as if People Mattered, E.F Schumacher, 1973, Blond and Briggs Limited.

> E. F. Schumacher was perhaps the first economist to question the ever-growing nature of big business and government. He proposed that some businesses should not seek to grow endlessly, gobbling up market after market for the sake of size

and power. What he was really describing was, I think, an early argument for capturing a niche market and staying within a company's core competencies. He also explained how smaller institutions can keep the human element in perspective.

Competitive Strategy: Techniques for Analyzing Industries and Competitors, Michael E. Porter, 1980, The Free Press.

This book, by a Harvard Business professor, is one of the few academic books I recommend. This serious, in-depth work on the economic elements and analysis of business strategies is not necessarily for the average small businessperson. Porter, perhaps the most recognized guru on strategy, emphasized large industries because this is the data he could study. I list this here more as a reference more than a must read book, for it helped me understand competitive strategy from an academic perspective.

In Search of Excellence, Tom Peters and Robert H. Waterman, Jr. 1982, First Warner Printing.

This famous book outlines "Lessons from America's Best-Run Companies," explaining why the best companies were at the time "the best." It was enormously popular among big business managers in the '80s and perhaps responsible in some ways for the deep jump into quality assessment and continuous improvement programs. Although it was an optimistic and noble endeavor, it missed the mark in many ways. If the companies that made the list of "Excellent" were really better, more of them would still be on the list today!

Still, it offers a basis for studying how even excellent (which does not mean successful) companies misunderstand their markets. It demonstrated how very large organizations, due to their size, can make decisions (or not make them) due to politics, greed and other issues of size.

Thriving on Chaos, A Handbook for a Management Revolution, Tom Peters, Alfred A. Knopf, 1987.

This book was intended to be a revolutionary jab in the side for every manager who thought he or she knew what was necessary to stay competitive. I like the radical aspects of the book, because it illustrated the level of shake-up that was then necessary in big business. The good news was that many small businesses already did many of these things. By shouting at management stuck in bureaucracy Peters probably cemented his brand with this book. In its unorthodox ramshackle way Peters pointed out some very important concepts that I built on in my practice. The most important was a five paragraph discussion of service that cited the highly impactful PIMS database.

The Millionaire Next Door, Thomas J. Stanley and William D. Danko, 1996, Simon and Schuster; and *The Millionaire Mind*, Thomas J. Stanley, 2000, Andrews McKeel Publications.

These two books explain the kinds of people who are millionaires, most of whom earned wealth through small business. My successful clients are very close to the profile described therein. Stanley and Danko do not provide rules; instead they point to the general behaviors of those who navigate the dangerous waters of small business. Emulating their characteristics can't help but improve the possibility. In most cases they also fit into the profile developed by Napoleon Hill.

The PIMS Principles, Linking Strategy to Performance, Robert D. Buzzell, and Bradley T. Gale. 1987, The Free Press.

This book is hard to find, and while it contains to me the most definitive support to my arguments and to my own chapter on PIMS, it is also a dry and academic book.

Generations, The History of America's Future, 1584 to 2069, William Strauss and Neil Howe, 1991, William Morrow and Company.

This 500 page book has greatly influenced my understanding of demographics as these apply to market niches. A book that has been enjoyed by many, it never gained a foothold in marketing circles or long term business planning. Yet it foretold many of the decisions and events that are now happening, based on different generation's approach to tough circumstances.

*The Science of Success, Charles G. Koch, 2007, Koch Industries Inc.

A remarkably concise discussion of value, Koch is a real authority, having created the largest privately owned company that has been built essentially in a single generation. While Koch's value diagram does not include my four elements, it would be better if it did! He does reference image, and does not discount it, but because his businesses use mathematical models to compare value, he apparently doesn't try to measure it. I believe this is a shortcoming, but in all other ways, he supports my understanding about creating quality, service and low price; and he proves that it works.

Marketing Aesthetics: The Strategic Management of Brands, Identity, and Image, Bernd Schmitt and Alex Simonson, 1997, The Free Press

This is a good supplement to Koch. Schmitt and Simonson articulate what I have felt about image and aesthetics since reading the *Visual Dialog*, in art school at the University of Colorado. They demonstrate how brands and aesthetics impact the financial outcome of businesses, and provide inspirational examples on how you should value your image more.

The 22 Immutable Laws of Marketing, Al Ries and Jack Trout, 1993, Harper Collins, N.Y., N.Y.

If you read just one marketing book in your life, this would be it. Short, simple, and right on, these are the marketing principles that I try to teach clients, and that, along with the PIMS Principles, are the basis of my Burgess Value Diamond and Crack in the Market philosophy.

From Good to Great, Jim Collins, 2001, Harper Collins.

A break-through book on leadership in large companies, it is notable because it does *not* describe successful small business owners very well. While many successful small business owners have some characteristics of the better leaders described by Collins, many without these qualities also are successful in small business. Like many companies described by Collins, small businesses do have the focus and honesty to emulate the Hedgehog concept, but being more patriarchal perhaps, or because small businesses learn to do what they can with who they have, they do not often "kick people off the bus," which Collins prescribes in "Getting the Right People on the Bus." Many small businesses have a higher moral ethic than the harsh reality of heavy competition among its workers. Amazingly they can still amass wealth in this manner.

I also recommend a variety of books by the three top market positioning authors, Jack Trout, Al Ries, and Stevin Rivkin. This includes: *Focus, The Future Of Your Company Depends On It*, by Ries; *The New Positioning*, by Trout and Rivkin; *Marketing Warfare*, by Ries and Trout; and *Bottom Up Marketing*, also by Ries and Trout.

The Triple Package: How three unlikely traits explain the rise and fall of cultural groups in America, by Amy Chua and Jed Rubenfeld. This book global looks at highly successful people in the U.S. and what cultures provided to them as preparation and drive to succeed. While it does not focus on small business per se, it provides excellent insight as to why certain cultural groups seem to produce individuals that succeed at rates high above the average American. This is a great read and study on America's greatness, failings and why.

Many additional books exist on the execution of marketing communications, known by insiders as MarCom. These books cover the specifics of direct mail, advertising, email and Internet marketing, events and public relations, etc. While I have learned from many of them, none is earth shattering. In fact, each explains a craft that fits under the strategy level of marketing. What is problematic is that many use these tools as if they could work without strategy. Since the tools will not help if the strategy is wrong, I leave them off the list.

About the Author

Ron Burgess is a long time business consultant, writer and speaker with deep expertise in small business marketing and management. As a young man, he built a specialty retail chain and small leather manufacturing company in Colorado.

Working for a national consulting firm, as divisional director for new product development and research, he was privy to hundreds of businesses throughout the U.S., where he learned first-hand how and why some were successful. In 1989, he started his consulting practice which continues today. In 1999 he co-founded a successful web development and marketing fulfillment company.

He holds degrees from the University of Colorado in both Fine Arts and Business.

Ron has worked for decades with businesses that continue to make their owners wealthy and that, despite the recession, have grown and prospered because they managed to find and defend their "crack in the market."

Follow Ron:

Twitter @RonBurgess
linkedin.com/in/**ronburgess**
www.FindingYourCrack.com
Check this website for updates, and sign-up for Ron's blog

.

Published by www.RedFusionMedia.com

www.ingramcontent.com/pod-product-compliance
Lightning Source LLC
Chambersburg PA
CBHW060005210326
41520CB00009B/830